Conversations With Angels
Volume I

Raise Your Inner Vibration
Mentally and Emotionally

^{the} Angel Lady Terrie Marie, D.Ms.

Copyright © 2018 the Angel Lady Terrie Marie, D.Ms. All rights reserved. No part of this publication may be reproduced or transmitted in any form or by any means, electronic or mechanical, including photocopying without written permission of the Publisher. Any unauthorized use, sharing, reproduction, or distribution is strictly prohibited. It is illegal to copy this book, post it to a website, or distribute it by any other means without permission from the Publisher.

Cover Design by Tovar Printing El Paso, Texas

Book Formatted by Bluebobo

Distributed by
Angel Lady Aurora, LLC
El Paso, Texas Unites States
© 2018 – All Rights Reserved WorldWide

Limits of Liability and Disclaimer of Warranty:
The Author and Publisher shall not be liable for your misuse of this material. This book is strictly for informational and educational purposes only.

Dedicated to ~

My Family and Friends for your unwavering
support and encouragement

Students and Clients for giving me the gift of sharing
my knowledge and experiences with you

LightWorkers and Healers I have met along the way
Mentors, Teachers and Coaches who have helped me
stand in my truth of who I am and
what I came here to do …

and to

My beloved Angels and Divine Source
~ the **Angel Lady Terrie Marie, D.Ms.**

the Angels Lady's Mission Statement: Success and Prosperity Seeking Spiritual Business Owners and Empaths hire me to help them blast through subconscious patterns of resistance and **dissolving negative self-talk are KEY steps** in clearing your path to being seen and magnetic. Following their Inner GPS, her clients get clarity they need to live their dreams doing what they love most, in miraculous ways.

Contents

Preface 1

Archangel Michael
Clearing Negative Energy 3

Angel Malkhiel
Angel of Inspired Creativity 11

Angel I'ahhel
The Quiet One 16

Archangel Sandalphon
Power and Glory of God; Answered Prayer 21

Archangel Raziel Secret of God;
Esoteric Wisdom and Knowledge 27

Archangel Taharial
Purity of God and Divine Protection 32

Angel Pathiel
The Opener 38

Angel Ezekiel
Angel of Transformation 43

Angel Nathaniel
Angel of Fire and Purification 49

Angel Meher
Angel of Reconciliation 54

Angel Gesele
Angel of Divine Life Purpose 59

Angel Domiel
Angel Prince of Majesty 65

Angel Uzzah
The Lord Is My Strength 70

Angel Jehudiel
Divine Direction 76

Angel Omniel
Oneness of Spirit 82

Gauri'el Ishlila
Angel Prince of the East 86

About the Angel Lady Terrie Marie, D.Ms. 93

Preface

Hello beautiful Soul,

This book has been two years in the channeling and writing. It was first started in January, 2016. It is now March, 2018. The Angels and I have channeled and written four Amazon Best-Sellers during these two years. This is the first of five Volumes each containing 16 Angel Conversations.

Conversations with Angels VOL I, is in Question and Answer format (Q&A). There is a short introduction for each Angels and then we get right into the Q&A discussion. All responses from the Angels begin with the Angels' name in **Bold** *and are n Italics* making it easy to distinguish my questions from the Angels' answers.

It has been an interesting adventure speaking with Angels this way. Yes, channeling Angels has become a part of my everyday way of living and being. Still, channeling in-depth conversations with each of these amazingly powerful Angels has and continues to be one of up-leveling my vibration and setting aside conscious mind Ego-chitter chatter on a daily basis.

There are to be an additional four volumes, each with 16 Q&A Angel Conversations. Each volume will be about 6 months or more in the channeling and writing. The Volumes will be on these topics:

- Volume II – Prosperity and Abundance
- Volume II – Love and Healing
- Volume IV – Manifesting Power
- Volume V – Inner Enlightenment

Due to the time and energy investment in making these writings available to all who are drawn to them, we, the Angels and I, have agreed that each Volume is to be released and published as eBook while the remaining Volumes are being channeled and written through me. Once all five volumes are completed, they will be compiled into one book. At this writing, the timeline is about 2 years more.

Much Love, Light, Peace and Purpose …
the Angel Lady Terrie Marie, D.Ms.

Archangel Michael
Clearing Negative Energy

Archangel Michael is the Divine Protector of small children, healers, and is the Patron for Soldiers everywhere. He protects you from negative energy within your thoughts, physical body and in your environment. He will cut negative energy attachments also referred to as Etheric Cords.

This mighty Archangel will clear your path, clear negative energy within and around you. He is capable of removing deep emotional pain, if you are truly open to receiving this gift of benevolent healing.

Hello Archangel Michael. It is an honor and a blessing to be speaking with you about this most important subject of protecting ourselves from negative energy.

Archangel Michael: *As it is with me also child, allowing me and my kind to speak through you reaching the many whom choose to hear and take notice of all that is being shared here among these pages.*

We shall commence with the teachings of clearing. Proceed with your many questions.

Thank you Archangel Michael.

We are often told about cutting negative energy attachments, freeing our energy bodies, raising our vibration from the inside out.

Archangel Michael: *Yes this is so, what is it you wish to understand further on this matter of truth?*

I wish to have a deeper understanding of how cutting cords affects our energy bodies, physical body and our Aura.

Archangel Michael: *Ah with this we shall begin at the beginning. Energy is much more fluid and yet it can also appear as non-moving or solid. Let me explain further.*

The body contains and is energy. The form of human is energy which has become matter and substance. The Earth Plane is comprised of dense matter or energy, therefore the form of the Human body has become form.

Therefore many things that have been created with thoughts and beliefs.

When beliefs change, new thought patterns are then released, creating form or shapes, into physical matter then accumulating into the form of substance.

As many have already spoken, there are infinite layers or vibrations of energy at various frequencies of sound and light.

There are so many frequencies of sound and light that are undetectable by or through physical eyesight, touch or hearing with physical ears.

Archangel Michael would you please help us understand how energy attachments, these etheric energy cords, both positive and negative, form and attach themselves to our physical body?

Archangel Michael: *Yes. It is best to receive explanation in this manner clarifying what can often be felt, but not see through physical sight.*

Allow me to explain in greater detail for all to grasp the subtle and at times, overwhelming power of these energy attachments upon the physical body.

Energy assumes shape, sound and light vibrating at both high and low frequencies.

All love based energies vibrate at higher levels of frequency which causes these emotions associated with love energy to be most elusive.

All fear based energies vibrate at much slower rates of frequency creating very dense, and at times very dark, heavy vibrations.

Negativity in all forms, no matter the reason, causes dis-ease, dis-harmony and imbalance on all levels of energetic vibration.

The heaviness of negative thinking and feeling energies pull down and backwards, higher vibrational energy frequencies.

Archangel Michael is this why it can often feel like an overwhelming pull backwards into the past and even prevent us from moving forward, even though this is what most Humans say they want freedom from negativity in all forms?

Archangel Michael: *Yes child this is indeed one of the many causes or reasons for such struggle often manifesting as defeat and failure.*

It being more clearly stated think of this backward pulling as mud or silt being filled with water energy sinking to the lowest depths possible.

It is therefore of paramount importance to nurture Human Spirit energy by calling forth through me, the destruction and dissolution of negativity in all its forms.

Is there anything more you can share with us about negative energy and how it affects every aspect of Human life as we know it?

Archangel Michael: *Yes. In this it is quite plain. Negativity breeds more negativity. Negativity creates a force of energy momentum much like a whirlpool or funnel shaped dark, violent winds that which you call tornados.*

These energetic phenomena are the physical manifestation of fear and doubt, despair, feelings of betrayal and much more.

So many blame untold numbers of others for their misfortunes causing the manifestation of negative energy to assume massive velocity causing massive destruction.

How does this relate to negative energy cords that attach to our physical bodies, Archangel Michael?

Archangel Michael: *Ah yes the next piece of this elusive puzzle of energy and its effects on the Human form.*

Alright then we shall proceed in this manner so all may have a clearer understanding of the magnitude of energy exchange. We shall begin with Human to Human attachments.

Let us begin further back with a familiar element necessary to all forms of life, water. There are Humans who have studied the phenomena of water absorbing, flowing freely and assuming the shape of its container.

Yes, Archangel Michael, one man, Dr. Masaru Emoto, has conducted extensive scientific studies of the power of negative and positive words and emotions on water molecules. The effect of hateful or negative thoughts and words produces distorted images of water molecules while positive, loving thoughts and emotions produce exquisite, intricate and delicate shapes of beauty.

Archangel Michael: *This is much the same effect of words, thoughts and emotional deeds of one Human upon another Human both positive and negative.*

Energy is free flowing attracting and being magnetized to like or similar vibrations or energetic frequencies.

It has been said many times by many teachers and leaders --- like attracts like --- for this is a Universal Truth., it is Law for it is unwavering.

Energy is free flowing both to its lowest and to its highest points much like water being an element whose shape is determined by the vessel which contains it. Can you begin to see through this perspective with more clarity?

Yes, Archangel Michael I can. Thank you.

Archangel Michael: *What else child do you wish to understand on this matter?*

Well, since you asked. Please describe with as much detail as words will allow, the effects energy, both positive and negative, have on the physical body, all our energy bodies and our Aura. I feel it is very important for everyone reading this, to have a very clear understanding so they can become more consciously aware of what energy does to their bodies and their inner-vibration mentally and emotionally.

Archangel Michael: *Well stated child. We shall dissect as much as possible using the best choice of words to accurately portray all that you have asked.*

Imagine and think of a pipe as a tube of light energy. Darkness represents that which is heavy, filled with fear, sadness, anger, resentment and even heartbreak at the deepest levels of emotion known to mankind.

Okay, I am imagining this. I see a rusty pipe with holes where water or light energy is leaking. It is dark and very heavy.

Archangel Michael: *Now child, imagine how this filth invades and infects your physical body spreading and flowing into all arteries within you. Can you see how darkness and shadow permeate and invade, causing destruction, manifesting physical symptoms of dis-ease?*

Yes I can. It looks like a river of black filth.

Archangel Michael: *If not contained and transformed it will cause damage manifesting in numerous ways such as lack, in all manners.*

Archangel Michael, would you please be more specific how or what kind of lack becomes manifested within and around us?

Archangel Michael: *Good. This is good for clarity so many may begin transforming where they currently find themselves, knowing there is so much more waiting for them.*

More specifically, negative energy literally invades the very cells and DNA structural strands of the Human form.

Negativity causes many to feel powerless to change circumstances. Many feel trapped, seeking to blame others for circumstances in which they find themselves presently.

Negative light energy causes physical health issues, lowers inner vibration, attacking that which is not wanted or desired.

Negative energy whether in thought of emotions causes distress, fear of loss which in turn causes and creates energetic blocks to receiving your Divine Birthright --- love, happiness, prosperity and abundance, contentment and the ability to fully express your purpose from the Soul level of knowing in its purest form of love and light.

And the positive effects of light energy on our physical and energy bodies Archangel Michael?

Archangel Michael: *This should be quite apparent yet we shall examine that which you have asked child.*

The exact opposite from the sludge of dark, heavy negative energy is the effect of positive, loving, compassionate light energy upon the physical body.

To be more precise in the language of words, the Soul experiences through the physical body, a sense of peaceful contentment.

Let us once again imagine the pipe or tube of light energy filled with the color of deep pink roses in fullest bloom exuding, projecting and radiating love energy in all directions throughout the physical body.

On all levels there is a semblance of harmony, peace and contentment. In this state of loving compassion all things manifest more quickly and with less effort.

Does this answer your questions?

Yes, but you would please break it down so that there is no confusion as to what you are so generously sharing with us?

Archangel Michael: *Yes. As you wish it, it becomes so for it is* law. The vibration of thought, word and deed manifest like, matching desires of the heart turning, churning and ultimately transforming light energy into substance and matter.

Archangel Michael, please give a few specific, tangible examples.

Archangel Michael: *Ah ... in the asking it is received. Love energy soothes the Soul. It creates space for healing and comfort. Love energy --- that which is positive on all levels of vibration --- permeates every cell, the very strands of DNA.*

Child, have you not witnessed such transformation within your physical vessel as a conduit of this work?

Yes, Archangel Michael, this I have. This work, like speaking with you here and now, raises my energy and my vibration beyond what I have previously experienced. Sometimes my physical body requires a time of rest so that I may once again re-align mentally, emotionally, energetically and Spiritually.

Archangel Michael: *Yes, this you have done many times and many times yet to come. Yet, most often for you it becomes as effortless as opening a new doorway and stepping forward, is it not?*

Yes. And at other times I require, or my physical human-self requires more time to re-align.

Archangel Michael: *This should now be sufficient. Let us now move to the cutting of negativity, removing and dissolving it from the inside out.*

The removing of these negative energy attachments, simply releases the physical body from continuously exchanging unwanted negativity.

This is a subject of which you are most familiar, teaching as many as will listen, taking heed of that which is taught through you.

How can we remove and dissolve these negative energy cords?

Archangel Michael: *It is in the asking child. There is no need for difficulty. When asked, it is done.*

Archangel Michael how shall we ask you for your help in removing unwanted negative energy cords or energy attachments?

Archangel Michael: *Here are my words --- Archangel Michael most powerful protector, please remove all unwanted negativity from within, on and around my physical and all energy bodies. Thank you.*

The asking completes the doing. In the doing, trust and faith create the knowing all is well.

In the asking and knowing, you create a force-field of Blue-White Light surrounding and protecting you from further negative energy infection.

If this is truth, Archangel Michael, why do we have to keep asking and continue to cut cords?

Archangel Michael: *Because child it is the way of humans to question that which appears before them in its simplicity. Fear and doubt creep in through human Ego-chatter. This is not condemnation, it simply is.*

All may ask as often as wished for in the asking all is answered, it is Law.

We are complete.

Thank you Archangel Michael.

Archangel Michael: *You are most welcome we shall move on from this point. The rest await you.*

Angel Malkhiel
Angel of Inspired Creativity

Malkhiel is an Angel of Inspiration and Creativity. Everyone has within them the Spark of Creation itself. When we are inspired by nature, music, a book we are reading or a beautiful painting, we are connecting with that inner-spark of creativity that is a natural part of us. Somehow we were taught or scolded into turning away from living from our imagination when we were young and free to play, making what we "saw" in our minds real.

Hello and welcome Angel Malkhiel. Thank you for being here and speaking with me today.

Angel Malkhiel: it is indeed a pleasure to be here with you speaking on this most important subject of inspiration and creativity. Shall we begin then with the questions as they form in our ensuing discourse?

Yes. What exactly does it mean to be inspired?

Angel Malkhiel: To be inspired is to be connected directly with that oneness deep within that space that bridges your heart center with that of your Soul Light.

It is following the spark that causes joy. It is being willing to follow your bliss no matter the naysayers. It is surrendering what others would say to your face or behind you.

Inspiration is that Spark of Knowing that all is unfolding simply in saying "yes" to what you have been called to do in that moment.

It is about being filled from within, allowing guidance to flow into your heart through the sub-conscious, tapping into the vast wealth of the Collective Unconscious Mind, that which is Universal.

Angel Malkhiel, would you please enlighten us as to how we can connect with that inner part of us that yearns to be inspired?

Angel Malkhiel: *Yes. This is much less difficult than is believed. It is accessed in the silence. It is accessed in those moments much like this when the focus is on connection rather than the lack of it.*

It is in those moments of extreme focus on another subject entirely, when a question has been answered, insight given, clarity achieved.

In being willing to let go of what is believed to be real, can those who seek these seemingly elusive moments of inspiring messages that ignite the spark of courage to move forward regardless of fear or trepidation.

Thank you. How closely related are inspiration and creativity? Or are they one and the same?

Angel Malkhiel: *They are indeed inseparable as well as complete unto themselves.*

Creativity in its purest form can and often does tap directly into the sub-conscious, pulling from its vast resources of knowledge and experiences. Those moments of clarity are about all that can unfold with each step along the pathway that opens before those who choose to heed their inner-calling to serve.

Angel Malkhiel there are so many who think and feel they are not creative because they are not artists or musicians. What would you say to these beautiful Souls to help them tap into their creativity?

Angel Malkhiel: *Every desire is borne from the well-spring of creativity. Yes, there are those among you who are more expressive through the arts of paint and music.*

There are still countless others whose creativity serves in many more subtle ways such as through the numbers and even the many forms of technology, which seemingly changes from one moment to the next.

Every idea to do things differently has sprung from a seed of desire which in turn is borne through creativity of thought and emotion.

Most consider this to be much more difficult and challenging to ignite and access within themselves which creates frustration where there need be none.

Most of us have a deep desire to figure out and fulfill our purpose. It is easier to imagine living the life we came here to live, if we can first "see" the vision that we feel compelled to pursue. How do we turn our thoughts and feelings into a vision or dream with the gift of inspired creativity?

Angel Malkhiel: *Ah child this is indeed a good question as it delves below the surface to uncover that which is natural when very young. There is much talk about being responsible, keeping one's feet on the ground, that flights of visions within the mind are dis-counted as not possible until there is truly little remaining of one's natural ability to "see" far beyond what is known.*

Most children play with what are to those who cannot see, referred to as "imaginary friends" when in reality, we from this Realm, are by your side every moment of your days.

To make this more plain, one must be willing to see as if for the first time, through the eyes of a child. This is what is meant to have the faith of a child.

Did you not "see" only to be told it was not possible by those who could not see nor could they allow you to "see" what they could not?

Yes. When I was in the 4th grade, an artist was visiting our school. She came into our classroom and gave us drawing lesson and told us to choose something in the room to draw, drawing *ONLY* what we saw.

I was excited to be given the freedom to play. I was drawing what I saw which was a vase of flowers with a pretty painted tray behind it. The lady artist told me that I was drawing something that was not there and to look again, to draw only what I could see and nothing more. Smiling, I looked again and saw the vase of flowers and the tray behind it, whole and complete. She kept telling me I was drawing something that wasn't there, that it couldn't possibly be seen from where I was sitting.

It wasn't long before I could no longer "see" what I "saw" just moments before. I lost all interest in the drawing. It was the beginning of disconnecting from my inner-self.

Angel Malkhiel: *Yes, in those moments so much is lost because those who have become "blind" to their inner-sight connection seek to have others conform to their ways rather than attempt to re-ignite their inner-sight.*

For all who read these pages, take heed to go within, seek that which has been temporarily misplaced.

I stay away from re-enforcing the notion of having lost creativity for it is not lost. It is merely dormant and can be re-ignited if the desire is true.

Is there anything else child?

No, unless there is something you would like to share with us.

Angel Malkhiel: *Only this and then we must move on as others await their voices to be heard.*

Even in death, there is creation. Creation is the very crux of all that is and has been created. All are created through thought, emotion and action. How then can any say they are not creative? If all would cease comparing themselves to the way others express themselves, more would certainly free themselves and the creativity which seeks to inspire greatness within the minds of all.

Thank you Angel Malkhiel this has been most enlightening.

Angel Malkhiel: *You are most welcome. We are now complete.*

Angel I'ahhel
The Quiet One

I'ahhel is the Angel of Meditation and quiet solitude or Sitting in the Silence so we can "hear" the soft, subtle messages filled with the answers and guidance we want and need to help us along our path.

Hello and welcome Angel I'ahhel I am looking forward to your insights beyond what most of us already know about the importance of meditation.

Angel I'ahhel: *it is with great pleasure to speak with you in this manner as there is greater need for more silence within and without.*

Before we go any further, please explain what you mean by "within" and "without."

Angel I'ahhel: *Yes, most certainly child. In the silence it is easier to hear that which must be heard to connect with the desires all keep buried deep within their heart-center.*

The "within" I refer to, as do we all, is that which causes and encompasses all to go within themselves through the inner-silence also referred to as self-reflection and introspection.

That which is not "within" is "without" that inner-self connection. "Without" is not connected to that which is "within" or to Source.

Is this understood more clearly or is there a need to delve deeper yet?

No, that feels complete. Thank you.

Why is it so important for us to meditate, to actually sit in the silence every day?

Angel I'ahhel: There is so much noise both within and without the conscious mind it is often difficult if not near impossible to hear with any true clarity that which is being given to you for your Spiritual Path.

Sitting in the silence creates space for that which you seek through your many questions, to be received.

Sitting in the silence releases emotional and mental pressure, giving the physical body a respite from carrying its many burdens.

If the hands are always filled to capacity as it is with the minds of many, how then can anything new and desired be picked-up and held? It simply cannot.

Something, whether it is a thought or emotion, must be set down upon the ground before anything new or desired can be fully received and accepted.

What you have just shared with us I'ahhel, is a concept I teach my clients and students. Now, perhaps more people will have a better understanding of the benefits of being in the silence.

For many, as soon as they close their eyes, Ego-chitter chatter starts to flood the conscious mind making it almost impossible to sit in the silence for even a few minutes.

Meditation for so many is simply a struggle and they soon just give-up feeling defeated. What can you tell us about the benefits of being in the silence beyond releasing stress and tension?

Angel I'ahhel: It is in the silence that all of creation was created with such stunning beauty everywhere the eyes could see.

The silence creates a vacuum for that which is desired to be birthed and given wings to fly. It is in the silence or within alignment of all things, that gives rise to inner-desires to make a difference.

So many on their path desire deeply to make a lasting, marked difference, yet they do not tend to their own needs within themselves.

Many of the known benefits are as follows:
*releasing stress and tension
*healing the body, mind and Spirit
*creating a dream that transcends current circumstance
*to hear, see and sense guidance that is being given

Yet many simply refuse to practice even a few moments each day cycle to be in the silence.

It cannot be stressed nor impressed too greatly, the necessity for calm quiet within the space of the conscious mind each of your days.

There is so much noise in your world at this time, it is near impossible to discern the difference between what is a truth and that which is not.

It is in the silence all of creation became manifested into physical form. How, then is it not the same with the dreams of the many who seek a better way to live in this world at this time?

Please I'ahhel, help us understand more about how creation is conceived and then ultimately manifested into physical form, change is reality as we know and understand it.

Angel I'ahhel: Yes, this is a most elusive concept at times simply because there is so much that is instantaneously acquired through the touch of a button without effort.

If there is much too much distraction in the form of memories in thought and emotion from the past, borrowing from that *which has yet to become present, there is little to no room for the conjuring of that which is deeply desired.*

Your Thomas Edison nor your Einstein would have been able to fully receive with the noise of current reality all around you. There must be time for the silence to see beyond the moment, to seeing beyond the struggle and strain of maintaining balance and alignment.

From the seemingly vastness of nothingness, comes all things great and small for the purpose of furthering and bettering life as it is now known.

Does this now fill the void of understanding the fullness of the void which so many view as an utter waste of their precious time?

Yes, I believe so, but I'd like to know more about how life and ideas are created in the silence.

Angel I'ahhel: *In the silence, the great void of noise and clutter of the conscious mind, the deepest reservoir of the great depths of the sub-conscious mind rises above many things, thoughts or notions of what first appears to be impossible in the light of the day and in the darkest of the nights.*

You have experienced many dark nights in which your will, commitment and all you believed to be truths were challenged and shown to you as more illusion.

Each time you chose to remain to face that which is indeed a falsehood among the many truths of this, your world.

This is very true. There have been times when experiencing a dark night so dark and so black, I did not think there would ever see light again.

Angel I'ahhel: *And yet, here you are continuing your work as never before with more clarity and conviction than you ever thought possible. Is this not so?*

Yes I'ahhel this is so. I did go through such an experience not so long ago. I literally died a death of such deep transformation; I am no longer the same in many ways. In other ways I am, admittedly, still feeling my way through with each step forward.

It was in the silence, even in those darkest of dark moments, which stretched into weeks, that I was able to truly shed the energetic skin that I used to hide the truth who I am and what I came here to do.

Angel I'ahhel: *Now child, you would never have been able to attain the knowing, the insights nor the strength required to fulfill the purpose being asked of you had you not cleared away all that no longer served you or your purpose, that which you agreed before the coming into this realm.*

This is true, I did a go through a type of death so that I could live more fully in the present moments, honoring all that came before.

I did, ultimately choose to step into the fullness of trust and faith to see the light, to see more clearly the vision of what's in front of me.

Every day I take time to being in the silence in ways that work for me. It is now part of my reason for being here to teach others the way into the silence is truly the way up and out of their current circumstances to a better life and way of fulfilling their purpose.

Angel I'ahhel: *Yes. This then, is now complete for in the telling there is little else to speak of now about the importance ... nay, the essential necessity of not only being but also remaining in the silence for extended moments of time.*

To see clearly, to feel clearly, to hear clearly, to sense clearly, to know clearly, one must be willing to go into the silence leaving all else behind.

Thank you I'ahhel.

Angel I'ahhel: *You are most welcome we are now complete. There is another who awaits your attention child. Go in peace, relish the silence.*

Archangel Sandalphon
Power and Glory of God; Answered Prayer

Archangel Sandalphon is one of only two Angels who were once human, like you and me. His biblical name is Elijah. This all powerful Angel weaves our prayer requests into a Garland, carrying them straight to the heavens.

He helps us be mindful, to have faith that our prayers our heard and answered before the asking leaves our lips. All that is asked of us is to be open to receive what we have asked for.

Hello and welcome Archangel Sandalphon. We are blessed with your presence on this day. There are many questions to ask about prayers and how or why they seem to go unanswered.

Archangel Sandalphon: *Indeed child this is our right moment of connection. It is I who am blessed in the giving of many sought after answers for there are indeed many that await the asking and the answering. You may begin this litany of questions.*

Thank you Archangel Sandalphon.

Archangel Sandalphon: *You are most welcome. Shall we begin then?*

Yes. If all Angels hear our prayers and requests for guidance and healing ... please share with us how you help us.

Archangel Sandalphon: *Yes. It is in the focusing of your thoughts, I am able to infuse powerful energy to carry your words, thoughts and prayers forward to all Angels being called upon by all who seek guidance and messages of healing.*

In the asking all is answered. There are no exceptions. No request carries more importantance than another yet this is the feeling many carry within the energy of their requests.

It is upon me to help all believe they are heard. It is upon me to assist all who ask to know they are heard and their askings will be answered in time.

I say all is answered in time simply because so many of your humankind feels unworthy or tainted by past situations and experiences. They question whether or not to ask for themselves.

Many have no issue to ask for others and often discount their deep-seated need to be heard and healed of all they carry within their hearts and minds.

The saddest thing for me and my brethren, is knowing there are so many in pain and yet they refuse to reach out to those among you who can genuinely help. Nor do they reach out to me and my brethren.

We, none of us, harbor any ill-will towards any human no matter where they have been or what they have done to themselves or one another.

How can we focus on our thoughts, emotions and energy to re-claim our personal power when we feel lost or confused about what the nest step on our path is or if we are even on the right path?

Archangel Sandalphon: *In the asking all is answered. In this there is no exception. The delays occur due to the blocking, feeling less than worthy of receiving that which has been asked.*

Would you please be more specific? Speaking for myself, when

I have been experiencing a Dark Night of the Soul, it feels like everything has or is in the process of falling apart around and especially within me. Many times I have felt alone and abandoned.

Archangel Sandalphon: *Ah child. There is indeed a sense of purging all that has come before, bringing you to this moment of extreme purging.*

All previous actions, thoughts ... all is questioned as nothing new fits where you are now traveling. The Spiritual Path for all Light Workers is treacherous. One can lose their footing from one moment to the next.

The truth being, all is being dismantled, making way for that which has been requested and longed for. In these darkest moments, the light is indeed the brightest. It is also a truth, that being in the midst of the darkness creates a filter of temporary blindness for the intensity of the light is great, the eyes must adjust as does the heart.

Please help us understand why some of our prayer requests are answered almost immediately while others seem to be a very long in coming or never get answered at all.

Archangel Sandalphon: *Yes. There is much confusion between linear, human time and Divine Time. Many brush off the denial of not receiving that which they desire as not meant to be or it will occur when it is time.*

While this is truth, it is also false. All create their own sense of Divine Time having been decided within their own energy. Meaning, if one does not feel worthy of receiving that which they ask, they shall not ever receive.

Closed minds, closed hearts determine the arrival of all things, opportunities. Is this not reflected in the way of things in your Earth walk child?

Yes. For a long time, I believed that no matter what I did, how hard I prayed or how much healing I did, it was never truly enough.

At the core of all things for me in this human life, was the fear of abandonment. I did for a long time, and I am ashamed now to admit this openly, that many times I felt my beloved Angels had abandoned me too.

Now, of course I clearly see and know it was me abandoning myself of out fear of being disappointed or failing to live up to what was being expected and asked of me. As I speak with you now Archangel Sandalphon, I am aware I get to forgive myself a bit more.

Archangel Sandalphon: *In this you help others to find their way with more clarity and compassion.*

Thank you.

Archangel Sandalphon: *The journey you agreed to walk is not for the faint of heart. Many strive to find their way in this dense energy world of physical matter.*

There is so much negativity and strife in this time; more of my brethren seek ways to reach the multitudes who truly seek a better way in walking the path before them.

Please help us know how to accept who we are and what we came here to do with compassion and humility.

Archangel Sandalphon: *Let us first address humility for many misunderstand the truth of this.*

Humility in all its genuine truth is the whole, complete acceptance of who you are and what you came here to do on this planet in this realm at this time of Earth's Spiritual evolution.

Please explain.

Archangel Sandalphon: *It is in the knowing, experiencing the Oneness of Self, Soul and Spirit that removes all traces of false humility and that of pride. It is in the knowing that all is an agreement between the Heavens, Source and each individual walking their path.*

In the walk along the Spiritual Path, much is shown, much is revealed as one is open to receiving knowledge of gifts given to be of service first to the Self and then to others and community.

The Self is to be attended to first. It is in the tending of Self that all is given to walk the path before you in service to others who also seek the light of Oneness and that of the Lord thy God. Do not mistake false humility, for below the surface is Ego pride which demands great attention.

Now let us speak of compassion for the Soul craves avenues of healing in many different ways. Compassion is the understanding of what another is or has faced on their Earth walk. It is not the taking on of another's burdens, nor is it anyone's responsibility to carry or heal those who wish only to be taken care of.

Those who seek to take, are not deserving of compassion. They are not deserving of being given for the sake of given too.

Excuse me Archangel Sandalphon. That sounds confusing. We are to be and give compassion but only to those who deserve it? Doesn't everyone deserve to receive compassion?

Archangel Sandalphon: *No. Allow me to speak more clearly as this is a most important matter in the true understanding of compassion, child.*

Yes, thank you.

Archangel Sandalphon: *There are those among you who expect, and at times demand, they be given what they feel is their due for surely their need and want is greater for the hardships they have endured in this life.*

The giving of compassion through unconditional love and non-judgement is not only right, it is essential for awakening to ever higher-levels of vibration.

The giving of compassion when it is not appreciated nor wanted with a heart that is true, is a waste when there are untold others who do indeed have a genuine need and desire for healing.

Compassion is offering non-judgement of how any one person chooses to walk his or her path whether it be in the light or in the darkness.

Is this now understood in its fullness?

Yes, thank you. Is there anything else you want to share with us about how to raise our inner-vibration through prayer?

Archangel Sandalphon: *Indeed, yes. As has been spoken before me, in the silence all is released, given and exchanged for the wisdom of the ages.*

In the focusing on that which is wanted, much is given to aid in the process of what is called Spiritual Awakening among those who seek to seek to see and hear that which was given at the beginning of their Soul journey.

In the seeking, in the knowing, all is given without exception. It is then the responsibility of the seeker to see through an open heart, an awareness of seeing that which is given without reservation.

If you or any reading our words are not receiving that which is asked, they and you child, are to look within their heart space for therein lay the answers to lack and delay.

Always the answer to all is in the silence. Always the answer to all lie within the openness of one's heart-center and that of the conscious mind.

We are now complete.

Thank you Archangel Sandalphon.

Archangel Sandalphon: *You are most welcomed child. It is with great pleasure and reverence all has been given through you for the many.*

Archangel Raziel
Secret of God; Esoteric Wisdom and Knowledge

Archangel Raziel is the Angel of Esoteric Wisdom and Knowledge. Each one of has something that is now behind, in our past that we may wish hadn't happened or could be healed once and for all.

Esoteric Wisdom is Ethereal in nature, part of the Collective Unconscious or Divine Mind. Being able to tap into and access the ancient knowledge, we can learn how to re-set outdated, negative beliefs that no longer serve us or our highest and best good and in truth ... never did. This mighty, benevolent Angels helps us reconcile past life issues and integrate our shadow-self with grace and compassion.

Hello and welcome Archangel Raziel, I am excited to be speaking with you today! There is so much we humans tend to hold-on to when there is no need. I am eager to learn more about how to truly let go of the past and integrate my shadow-self with grace and compassion.

Archangel Raziel: *Let us begin then with your list of many questions. I too am looking forward to our conversation. There* are many who dwell for too long in the past, bringing so much unnecessary negative filth with them into their present. It need not be so.

Tell me, what shall we start with child?

What is it about the past or past lives that seem to haunt so many on their Spiritual Path?

Archangel Raziel: *The past, child, is a point of reference for Human Ego to continue showing lessons learned or that which needs yet to be learned and subsequently released for healing and reconciliation.*

It is not helpful when negative stories of the past are continually repeated, told over and over as if it were a new experience to be living now in the present moment. It is acceptable and advisable to retain lessons learned to avoid future encounters along your respective paths. Only in the releasing, can the Soul be freed from reliving that which is truly behind you.

Many hold onto past hurts as if they are victories or medals of merit won in battle. They are not. They are scars that mark the passing of time, the passing through healing and ultimate integration.

How can we truly release very painful experiences and ultimately integrate them without reliving the past? Every time I think about a negative experience, it feels as if it is happening all over again. How can we reconcile and integrate without continuing to reinforce the negativity?

Archangel Raziel: *When there is truth in healing from the heart-center without prejudice, non-resistance and without judgment, the lesson learned remains a guidepost as one moves forward. In this way, the past is laid to rest without re-engaging that which is no longer wanted.*

Please explain, because we're taught that we need only be willing to forgive those who have wronged us for the process to begin.

Archangel Raziel: This is indeed so child. There need only be a willingness to be open to forgiving those who have trespassed against you. Yet this is only the beginning as there must be genuine healing at the Soul level beginning first with the heart-center, that which houses all human emotions of love and hate.

Is this now understood?

Yes.

Archangel Raziel: Then let us continue to be more clear so that all may understand the words shared here among these pages.

The next concept that craves clarity and simplicity is that of integration, bridging the past with the present, clearing the way for what awaits you on your Spiritual evolution ever upward in vibration.

Integration in its truest form is a weaving of what once was, with the present moment mentally, emotionally and energetically.

It is as if a tapestry is being woven of light and dark and all shades in between, forming beautiful, brilliant patterns. When one looks up, all that is seen is jumbled, tangled knots and the crisscrossing of thoughts, emotions, relationships and experiences both positive and negative.

It is only in the weaving of what was and that which is, can that which is yet to come, be created with love, beauty and light. There will always be those among you who seek the darkness as their path. Yet, all who choose the pathways of light need not dwell in the shadows of others.

This sounds good, but how can we do this ... heal, release, reconcile and ultimately integrate so that we can experience balance and harmony in our present moments?

Archangel Raziel: Ah. I see now more clearly the dilemma of what has, thus far being shared here.

One must be willing to see the truth in all situations no matter the cause, no matter the outcome. One must accept their responsibility for all have shared in the making of what has or has not occurred.

One must be willing to let go of any remaining ill will towards another and themselves or the healing cannot progress towards ultimate integration. The act of integration is the accepting of that which occurred and that which did not. Nothing, nor anyone, can change what has already occurred. The present moment is an opportunity to create anew or re-live that which has already occurred. There is always choice.

It is the weaving of past and present creating a sense of oneness. Oneness is that which is whole, complete and perfect with its many flaws mixed with shadow and light.

There is nothing more to be said in this matter at this time.

Thank you Archangel Raziel. I now have a better understanding of integrating shadow and light. How does this help us reconcile past lives for those who have memories that have surfaced in this life?

Archangel Raziel: *It is much the same and yet so many cling to what once was as a way to avoid living in the now. Knowing what has come before is a gift to aid, to guide, in the present.*

Then, if I understand you correctly, being able to heal, release, reconcile and ultimately integrate positive and negative, shadow and light, past and present, is the key to experiencing a sense of empowerment and harmony, which helps us have balance in the present.

Do not harbor ill will towards others. Do not berate the self. This only causes more pain and sorrow to heal within the Soul's Earth Journey in physical form.

All that has been experienced as the Soul travels along its Earth Journey is now a part of the whole. Nothing can be erased nor should it be attempted as this only causes a time-memory warp, disturbing the present and future experiences, both positive and negative.

It is in the seeing; it is in the knowing, all has brought each of you to where you find yourself in this present moment, then the healing of integration can truly begin. The weaving of what once was and that which is, seeks balance within the harmony of aligning into Oneness.

There is only Oneness, regardless of outside appearances. The inner is to be first aligned in thought and heart, allowing all that remains to merge into that which is. Only when integration has begun can you truly move forward.

It is not enough to say these things; action must be taken to purge that which is truly no longer needed for the journey before you.

Use that which is past as a pathway guide into and through that which is before each of you. As you each step forward into the fullness of who you are, that which you came here to do will be revealed to you within each step forward.

Unless there are additional questions at this time, we are now complete in this moment.

No, Archangel Raziel there aren't more questions at this time. Thank you for being so open on this most important and somewhat mysterious subject.

Archangel Raziel: *There is always more, yet this will suffice for now in the place and time.*

We are complete.

Archangel Taharial
Purity of God and Divine Protection

Archangel Taharial helps us create Sacred Space within our inner-self and in our physical environment. When we have a "safe place" to open our hearts and bare our Soul, we can connect to Spirit, Angels and Divine Source.

Spirit, Angels and Divine Source are all part of the whole. Each is also whole and complete unto themselves, flowing one into another without end. In truth, there is no beginning nor is there an end, there is simply Oneness that is also referred to as the "the Collective Unconsciousness" or Divine Mind.

This amazing and incredibly benevolent and powerful Angel helps us rise above the obstacles and challenges we face along our respective paths.

He will shield us as we go within connecting with our Spiritual Path and find the courage to step out of the Spiritual Closet to accept who we are and what we came here to do with compassion, humility and grace.

Hello and welcome Archangel Taharial. It is an honor and a privilege to be connecting and speaking with you here and now.

Archangel Taharial: *It is I child who is honored to be able to share through you and this medium in your world of dense physical matter to speak of the importance of awakening here and now.*

There are untold multitudes who have yet to awaken to their inner truth and many others who are consumed with fear and choose to trudge along in their self-created miseries of illusion disguised as lack and limitation.

There are so many, who crave the light, yet shrink back into the shadows of feeling themselves unworthy, underserving of Divine Favor and Protection.

Many feel themselves to be unclean because of all that has or has not transpired in this, and all previous lifetimes here in this world.

This planet of Earth is among the most difficult and arduous journeys that any Soul chooses to undertake. There are many Souls who simply choose to leave before the agreed upon length of service honoring that which was set into motion just prior to the moment of transition from pure Spirit into physical form.

It is necessary to understand the moments just prior to physical conception in the womb of the one who is to be nurturer and caretaker, as they can the beginning of forgetfulness.

In some ways, all is stripped when traveling through the "veil" where all once was nothing and everything in the same moment. In its purest form, every Soul is One with the All, that which is Divine Source, the Great Collective Unconscious.

There are no wants of needs for all is instantaneously manifested within thought and emotion. All is conceived within unconditional love for there is only love and light. That is Pure Soul Essence ... Light, Unconditional Love and Oneness with the All.

Now child, what questions have you?

Before I ask the first question Archangel Taharial ... thank you for all you have just shared with us. I will need to come back to fully comprehend all you have so generously given.

Archangel Taharial: *You are most welcome. This is the purpose for our communicating in this manner, is it not?*

Yes.

Archangel Taharial: *Then let us begin. What shall you ask of me first?*

Please explain what it truly means to "step out of the Spiritual Closet" to connect or re-connect with our truth without causing distress or drawing undue attention to ourselves.

Archangel Taharial: *Let us begin by being crystal clear that for some, it is absolutely imperative that they be seen and heard for theirs is a message of healing, hope, transition and the promise of a better way filled with positivity rather than the dominance of negativity which is prevalent in your physical Earth world.*

For many others, all that is being asked is the acceptance of that which is. Within the Soul Memories, are the Truth, the Light and the Way.

To be clear, all that is being asked of the many, is to walk their path with integrity, re-aligning that which is now in physical form and that which remains connected energetically to the Collective Unconscious for all Eternity.

There are many worlds as there are many Realms. Each has its specific energy. There are few like that of your present world.

I digress as this is a subject for further study which is not our purpose for these communications now. The question at hand is finding the courage within, allowing the light within the Soul as it merges through the heart-center to be seen.

That which is kept hidden in the shadows suffers needlessly, yet many will choose to stay hidden in the shadows seeking the safety of anonymity.

How can we protect ourselves from the darkness and the negativity from within ourselves and of course from others?

Archangel Taharial: *It is in the asking as it is with all that is wanted, needed and ultimately desired to fulfill the purpose for having descended into physical form.*

More clearly stated ask and you shall receive Divine Protection. The degree and depth to which the Shield of God's Purity is given, depends entirely upon the receptivity of the one who is asking.

Many ask immediately negating that which has been asked. When that which has been asked goes seemingly unanswered, it gives false testimony to a belief of unworthiness, not deserving of Divine Intervention in the form of Divine Protection. My shield surrounds not only the physical body but also the Aura.

All comes to choosing transcendence above that which seeks to anchor you in the shadows of darkness.

With each step forward, the Light within shines more brightly and in essence, blinding all those of lower vibration. That which is of equal vibration and those who seek their truth in the Light are drawn together. It is Law.

Ask that the Shield of Divine Protection and that of God's Purity surround you and all shall simply fall away from you and all who ask. It is simple. It is not at all complicated.

The Human mind is that which determines the ease or difficulty of all that is asked whether it be protection, guidance, healing or manifestation.

Once the decision has been made to step out into the Light, the true journey upon each unique Spiritual Path begins in earnest.

One can choose to turn back, turn a blind-eye or continue forward no matter what attempts to distract you from your chosen pathway.

What else are you to ask of me this day?

Most of us are familiar with the concept of creating Sacred Space within our physical environment by designating a room or a corner of a room for healing and meditation to connect with our inner-intuitive self.

How can we create and maintain Sacred Space within? Is this something we can do mentally or within our heart-center?

Archangel Taharial: *Yes there is much that needs to be made clear on this most important facet of creating Sacred Space within.*

Most have, including you child, have sought the advice, opinions and support of those whom they trusted with the deepest desires of living a whole life filled with purpose, harmony, joy passion and that of prosperity and abundance, yet the exact opposite was given.

Each time another dis-respects your inner-most desires to make a difference the way it is intended, the Soul retreats a bit farther into itself, protecting its precious mission to come forth at a point where there is a feeling of safety and protection from the multitude of naysayers.

Every Soul housed within a physical body comes willingly to shed light to thrive, fulfilling its sole purpose which is to be of service.

Nowhere is it written among the heavens that being of service to the Self and to your fellow humankind that those among you should give tenfold and in return receive little. When there is prosperity and abundance for one there is also prosperity and abundance for the many. It cannot be otherwise.

Another perspective is this ... how shall you live your purpose in its fullest measure if consumed by fear, worry and lack?

It cannot be so.

That which is like unto itself is drawn together with others of like mind and of equal or higher vibration. It is Law. It simply cannot otherwise be.

All who ask shall receive.

All who knock shall have doors opened before them.

All who seek shall find and be found.

It is Law. It bears repeating as it cannot otherwise be.

We are now complete with these communications. We have given much for the many with pleasure and reverence for each respective path. All must travel their path as it is revealed step-by-step.

None need travel alone.

Thank you Archangel Taharial. This has been insightful and enlightening.

Archangel Taharial: *As it is intended. We are now complete. My brethren await your attention.*

Angel Pathiel
The Opener

Angel Pathiel's primary purpose and specialty is helping us clear mental and emotional blocks that show-up both within our conscious mind and around us. Our conscious mind, what I also refer to as Ego-chitter chatter, creates obstacles along our Spiritual Path. Sometimes, these blocks appear when we least expect them.

This Angel, who is The Opener, assists us with healing mental and emotional obstacles from the inside out, clearing our pathway to imprint new positive beliefs, which will in time, become our truth.

Hello and welcome Angel Pathiel. I have been looking forward to communicating with you and today is especially significant ... at least for me because there is major transition in process in my life right now. Just yesterday, I was feeling scared, a bit anxious and angry because I was stepping off the edge once again.

Angel Pathiel: *Let us begin there, in that moment child. Tell a bit more, giving us all the foundation for the clearing of your* pathway as an ideal example for others to easily adopt for their specific needs.

Well, alright. This wasn't my intention. I am open however, so that others may learn from my journey.

It hasn't always been easy to accept who I am and what I came here to do which is help millions of women and men connect with their Angels to live their purpose with prosperity and abundance.

In the summer of 2015, everything came crashing down around me, almost overnight. There was a span of 5 weeks of intense, self-reflection, healing and regaining the will and courage to resume my path.

The ensuing 7 months have been all about being in trust and faith knowing that I am taken care of as I take care of myself in ways I never did or would before.

More recently, the final phase of healing, letting go and opening my heart and Soul even more, has begun. For a short time within the last 24 hours, fear and doubt reared its ugly energy.

By the grace of you and all my beloved Angels, one of my dearest friends and my own determination, the negativity was processed fairly quickly.

Earlier today, I read something that stopped me --- "Remember to come out of your cocoon once the transformation is done. Darshana Patel" --- this is exactly what it feels like … coming out of a cocoon.

How do we clear any lingering negativity in our thoughts and emotions so that we can fully emerge into the truth of who we are? Isn't this part of what it means to clear our pathway?

Angel Pathiel: *Yes, indeed this is so for all memories both positive and negative are part of the whole. There cannot, in this Earth world of physically dense matter, be only that which is solely negative, nor that which is solely positive.*

There is a sense of duality, light and dark, lack and plenty, feast and famine, poverty and prosperity. As with all things that which appears to be reality is that which is being focused upon.

In the face of adversity or dis-ease, there is always the polar opposite, to balance the outcome of any situation.

The misnomer is that for the masses, there is only lack, delay and limitation, which appears to those who experience the opposite of that which they desire to have, to be the only truth. What is seen is the perception of the rich getting more and those who are not, staying where they currently find themselves which is not at all where they truly want to be.

What is at stake is literally and figuratively changing their stars ... changing, forever changing their vibration from the inside out.

What most fail to understand through no fault of their own, is a hefty portion of what they feel and how they view the world around them is not their truth. These truths have been learned over many lifetimes, passed through to them and inherited from generations before them. I must state quite clearly, this is simply a way of releasing layers upon layers of learned behaviors that do not serve your highest and best good and that of your purpose of being here in this place and time.

How do we really get rid of these beliefs that we have inherited, so we can truly be free of the past?

Angel Pathiel: *This is good. Have you not healed this for yourself child, lighting the way for countless others?*

Yes. But it has been along and very difficult journey. For such a long time I didn't understand why it was such a challenge to heal beliefs that I just knew weren't mine especially since this is my only time incarnation into physical form to walk this Earthly path.

Isn't there an easier way to clear the obstacles that always seem to trip so many when things are beginning to manifest in positive ways?

Angel Pathiel: *Yes. The way and the path are made clear in the moment of the asking. Yet, the multitudes have so little trust and faith in receiving the absolution and subsequent healing they crave.*

Please be more specific. I would like to know more, making my own journey easier too.

Angel Pathiel: *Yes. Close your eyes, imagine before you a jungle, a beautiful tangle of exotic plants, trees, flowering bushes and vines all tangled and interwoven from neglect.*

Now imagine standing at a small clearing looking at all that is before you on this path. Be willing to see beyond the immediate tangle of growth that appears impassable. There is indeed beauty in the growth of trees, flowering bushes, plants and vines. There is also that which is no longer needed to remain lush and beautiful.

Now child, imagine the cluttered pathway begin to open before you clearing, allowing you to pass. Mindfulness is the first of many steps. The level of trust in yourself and in my brethren and me, dictates the ease, grace and speed with which the pathway is cleared, becoming less narrow with each forward step.

The Fear of the Unknown is the tripwire for many. You too, have experienced this very tripwire many times over. It is only recently that you, child, have been able to clearly recognize that which triggers fear within your thoughts, gripping your heart with doubt.

Yes this is true. I am handling these pesky energy walls or negative energy demons much better. It is easier, I call on Angels to help me and give myself permission to process and to sleep, allowing my physical self to heal, forgive and release the outcome of what is in front of me at the time.

I am also facing the fear with an open mind and an open heart. I write a letter to myself saying what needs to be said or written and then burn it, watching the flames release the energy with love and compassion.

In this way, I am giving myself a way to express what I'm feeling without holding onto the negativity in any form.

Angel Pathiel: *Yes. This makes perfect sense for things must be attended to in physical form as this is the way of Earth and its heavy, dense energy.*

Only when one allows the Self to fully release that which attempts to keep all in a never-ending cycle of negativity, can there truly be freedom from that which was never yours to carry.

This simple yet profound truth clears all obstacles, clearing your pathway to all that truly awaits you for the fulfilling of your purpose in this time and in this place among the many who seek a better way.

We are now complete for our purposes here and now.

Thank you, Angel Pathiel.

Angel Pathiel*: It is I who am honored to be included among these pages in an effort to assist the multitudes who seek freedom from that which distracts, clearing the pathway before them.*

We are complete. The next awaits you.

Angel Ezekiel
Angel of Transformation

Transformation is all about change, which for most of us can feel quite overwhelming and at times intimidating. Angel Ezekiel taught me, we need only change one small thing. He helped me see that it's like tossing a small pebble into a pond and watching the ripples keep getting bigger and bigger as they radiate outward from the center of where the pebble was first tossed into the pond.

When we are willing to change one thing --- one action, one thought, one belief --- we can literally cause everything in our lives to change just because it's not possible to change one thing, thought, belief or feeling and not have it affect everything else.

Angel Ezekiel helps us breakthrough old mind-sets and belief systems which in turn shifts our perception, enabling us to see, recognize and acknowledge positive, forward movement and opportunities as they "show-up" for us along our path.

Angel Ezekiel, hello and welcome. Thank you for being here. I just love the way your energy softly creates change in ways we are able to manage.

Angel Ezekiel: *Make no mistake child there are many instances in which some among you require winds equivalent to gale force winds for that is all they accept as being significant to warrant their attention.*

This is true. There have been instances that included me too because I just wasn't getting it.

Angel Ezekiel: *Yes, yet you have learned well. It is no longer necessary, for you are more attentive. There are still those moments in which you are so focused on the tasks at hand that several warnings are given to you.*

I agree.

Angel Ezekiel: *This becomes less and less. Now, shall we begin with your list of questions as I am here to be of service, a catalyst for massive change and transformation from the inside out, allowing transformation to radiate outward, affecting every aspect in the most positive ways possible.*

Thank you. I'd like to start by understanding more fully the concept of transformation and how changing one thing like a belief or choosing to re-connect with our inner-essence can really and truly create lasting change from the inside out.

Angel Ezekiel: *Ah this is indeed a perfect point of entry into so vast a subject as transformation. Again, change is inevitable to one's Spiritual Journey and that of fulfilling that which has been agreed upon prior to incarnation into the physical form you now find yourselves.*

This is more than a simple concept that of being willing to change, heal or surrender one thought. As one thought, for example, is given wings to fly out of the conscious mind, one creates movement. At first, in the beginning, this one thought seems to be a solitary thought and yet the movement of energy creates space for another thought to be transformed simply because the first is no longer the same.

Transformation is often seen as something that brings dis-

harmony, lack and limitation. Yet it can be ... if one is truly open to the many gifts disguised in the wake of movement ... incredible, powerful and rewarding.

The desire for change in the hearts and minds of the many is great yet that which is needed most, courage and inner-strength, requires forgiving and letting go of what no longer serves.

In the absence of negative energy, there is love, healing and growth. Many seek transformation without going within. This is the one true way to lasting alchemy, the very truth of massive change. If one seeks to change his stars, then one must be willing to re-arrange thoughts and emotions, creating a sense of emotional and energetic alignment.

I often tell a story to help my clients understand this concept because change can be overwhelming, especially when there is a Fear of the Unknown which causes resistance.

The story is about wanting space for a new set of linens. Just wanting to have enough space for a new set of bed linens is what sparks clearing and re-organizing. The intention is space and when we're finished finding "new space" most often we have found a few things we no longer need and other things are re-arranged and not only do we have space for the new linens, more than likely, there is more space in the linen closet than there was in the beginning.

Angel Ezekiel: *Yes, this is exactly so. You have captured the essence of transformation in the telling of this simple story.*

Is it really this simple when we want to release negative beliefs that have us blocked at every turn?

Angel Ezekiel: *Yes. In its simplicity, this is the path of profound transformation. Allow me to explain further.*

The Essence of all things seen and unseen, known and unknown are the exact same. Each begins with desire. Desire begets thought. Thought begets emotion. Emotion begets vibration. Vibration begets magnetic attraction. Magnetic attraction eventually transforms into that which has manifested physically.

For example, let us delve into relationships between two people. It matters not the nature of the relationship, it matters only for these purposes that there has been a rift of sorts through the hurting of pain and sorrow, mis-understanding or possibly deceit. In this instance, it is negativity which has been triggered creating an ever greater sense of negative emotional responses.

As the negative is focused upon, there is an increase in intensity. This intensity becomes an attachment or energy channel for continued exchange between all involved.

You child, have experienced such spurts of negativity when those you trusted with your dreams and your heart have suddenly shown the truth of who they are which revealed a shift in vibration causing a mis-match where there was a vibrational match previously.

This is true. Understanding the ways of others has, at times, left me feeling betrayed and at times even feeling abandoned, wondering why people do these kinds of things to each other and to themselves. How can we change our perception of what is or isn't happening in ourselves?

Angel Ezekiel: *In relation to what, child? Be more specific so we may be more forthcoming and of service to all who visit these writings.*

How can we change how we view something that is happening like when a trusted friend or partner suddenly does or says something that is the exact opposite of what has been experienced? How can we change how se see a sudden shift in direction or attitude?

Angel Ezekiel: *In relation to what is termed reality which is simply a reflection of thought and emotion, focused upon by one's conscious mind.*

Instead of seeing and feeling as if you are the one being attacked, mentally or emotionally, choose first to acknowledge what is felt in the moment. The second piece to this puzzle of perception transformation is to ask what the purpose for this occurrence is in relation to your Spiritual Path. One could take this further yet, asking what message is being given.

Many times what occurs is simply a sign of a vibration mismatch, signaling time of forward movement away from what was and towards what now becomes a more favorable vibrational match. Remember child, vibration seeks its own kind. Low vibrations attract the same. Those who are content at the lower ends of vibration remain there by choice because it feels easier to wallow in their muck, mired in the heaviness of negativity.

Others seek change to better themselves, finding others who accept them in their entirety without judgment.

Everything, then is truly all about going within first and creating space one thought and one emotion at a time?

Angel Ezekiel: Yes. This is exactly so. Massive change is always, always, always begun with a desire to feel differently. All change begins first with one being willing to surrender anger, hurt, betrayal. All begins with a sincere willingness to no longer remain the same, repeating sameness day-in and day-out. The sameness wears thin the Soul energy. It seeks love, compassion, nurturing. That which is its equal match vibrationally.

There are those among you who simply cannot progress beyond a certain level of energy because they are unwilling to heed messages received about their purpose of service.

Changing how we see something is a form of transformation too. Being willing to see a situation through a different lens or viewpoint is one way we get validation for our own inner Spiritual growth.

Angel Ezekiel: Yes, this is exactly so. You are perceptive in the ways of change. Your journey in this has been arduous and yet you have now arrived at this point along your pathway to where you are going. In this you have done exceptionally well.

Thank you, Angel Ezekiel.

Angel Ezekiel: *You are most welcome. If there is nothing more on this subject at this time, we are complete.*

This feels complete to me as well. Thank you.

Angel Nathaniel
Angel of Fire and Purification

Angel Nathaniel's fiery energy helps us dissolve, release and detach from the drama of others around us and from our own internal drama. It's all about helping us connect with our inner-self, replacing fear with the courage to transform and rise above every thought, emotion and action that isn't in alignment with our dreams and goals.

Angel Nathaniel helps us find contentment where we are, while we are purging negativity in all forms, creating space within, to step beyond our comfort zone and into that place of empowerment.

Angel Nathaniel, hello and welcome. It is not at all surprising that today of all days, this is the day for our conversation together.

Angel Nathaniel: *Explain so that others may also understand the significance of our coming together on this day.*

Yes of course. Just a few days ago an obstacle came into my path. It was so sudden and felt completely overwhelming I couldn't breathe. At this time or place along my journey, I am in the process of downsizing from a home I cared for and love for nine years. I'll miss the meditation garden the most.

Anyway, I reached out to my Spiritual family for prayer and healing support knowing if I wasn't mindful, this sudden turn of events would lead me down a rather dark tunnel. In less than 24 hours, not only were all issues resolved, all obstacles disappeared as quickly as they had appeared.

I do remember asking Angels to help me stay in trust and faith. There is no doubt that all the prayers and my beloved Angels helped me help myself to re-focus my thoughts and emotions for a positive outcome. The right and perfect new home for me and our work has manifested and all is well, despite surface appearances in those awful, few moments.

Angel Nathaniel: *I was among the many attending you child as there was massive release of negativity that initiated this current transformational cycle.*

Yours has been a journey of release, purging, healing and expansion many times over. Yet, none such as this cycle of transformational transcendence into knowing all is indeed provided to you.

Energy is neither good nor bad. In essence there is only energy which vibrates at various frequencies. Some higher, others lower. Energy frequencies attract that of like vibration.

Angel Nathaniel, that sounds confusing and quite clear all in the same moment. If I was very happy and my vibration was high, how then, can something or someone suddenly appear out of nowhere to cause such intense, negative reactions within us?

Angel Nathaniel: *This is a good question indeed. Allow me to be more precise in my explanations allowing for clarity, not confusion.*

Let us refer to your recent experience child. In this particular instance, there was another involved who did not live-up to his specific responsibilities causing a chain-reaction of unforeseen events.

In part you also caused this situation to arise in order to allow the physical manifestation of your desires. It was not through malice on the part of another nor on yours. With the situation taking a most unexpected turn, it allowed for the purging of fear of failure and reflection. It also released pressures you were unaware of because of your intense healing practices.

You were well aware the situation that presented itself was indeed not punishment, nor a sign of imminent disaster. Instead, you prayed, forgave and healed within a relatively short period of Earthly time. You approached the situation with compassion, unconditional love and humility. Thus the outcome you experienced, while better than your human Ego anticipated or expected, was what you requested so definitively.

That's very true.

Angel Nathaniel: *All has unfolded with great favor, as it was intended. No harm has resulted to any. You are where you are meant to be because of your countenance and open heart child.*

What else shall you ask of me now?

Yes, thank you. I am very grateful and appreciate the outcome and am humbled by the outpouring of support from my Spiritual family and my beloved Angels.

How can we detach from the drama that others attempt to drag us into? For some, it seems nearly impossible to escape the seemingly never-ending cycle of being sucked into situations we really want no part of.

Angel Nathaniel: *The way of detaching from human drama both within and around you, is not as difficult as is believed. It does require courage to stay removed from all who choose to dwell only in negativity.*

We humans fear being alone. We tend to accept disrespect and tolerate others treating us with unkindness through words and actions, cutting and wounding us deeply, yet we stay where we find ourselves. How can we overcome this?

Angel Nathaniel: *It is in accepting that not all who have chosen to incarnate are willing to let go and release all that not only does not serve them but also others who are unwilling to release themselves from such perpetual cycles of negativity.*

Once in a loop, it requires mindful sustainability to remain removed and detached, while remaining in that space of self-love and unconditional love for others, whatever their choices. Most believe if there is given enough patience and support, that all will come to see the light even in the midst of shadows.

That is not the chosen reality of the many. The Fear of the Unknown is far too uncertain; hence the multitudes who speak words of change yet remain exactly where they continually find themselves. The purging of fear, the detaching of drama has its consequences.

What are these consequences and if there are consequences to purging and detaching, why should we step into the unknown?

Angel Nathaniel: *There are what many consider dire consequences through detachment from negativity in any form no matter its origins ... consequences such as these ...*

* *breaking away from the known, whether it is desired or not*
* *thrust out into the known world all alone without those they consider supportive and loving*
* *the severing of familial ties, the leaving of friends behind them*
* *intense feelings of loss, shame or guilt for leaving family behind to follow their path of fulfilling their purpose*

What one fails to consider in its entirely, is the leaving of the Self where it cannot possible thrive in happiness or contentment, peace and harmony. Where one cannot thrive, the fulfillment of one's purpose un-hindered cannot come to pass.

No matter the choices, courage is required both in the staying and in the leaving.

Is there something you can share with us to help us help ourselves in moving away from people, situations and potential experiences that cause harmful drama and towards the light, even when we have no idea what is waiting for us Angel Nathaniel?

Angel Nathaniel: *Yes. Imagine my presence with you now and in those moments. My great wings enfold you with great compassion, all the while burning that which is no longer desired away and from within your mind and heart. The burning, is through one's willingness to release the Soul-Self from Earthly negativity, creating a sense of Heaven where you find yourselves in the moment.*

This willingness is to be accompanied with forgiveness. Forgiveness of Self and all involved. The only sustainable agreement is that which is conceived in forgiveness, compassion, love and genuinely humility.

Is there more you wish of me at this time? All has been said. That which is not wanted can be released through detachment and the purging of thoughts and emotions.

No. Thank you for being here with us sharing your wisdom and guidance Angel Nathaniel.

Angel Nathaniel: *It is I child who thanks you and all with whom you share the journey among the many who choose to remain mired in the shadows of darkness.*

We are now complete.

Angel Meher
Angel of Reconciliation

Reconciliation is the conscious act of integrating two or more facets of ourselves into a state of Oneness. Being willing to accept aspects or facets of ourselves that are both light and shadow, is the first step in truly releasing ourselves from the past, creating space to move forward, feeling and being whole and complete.

Angel Meher gives us the gift of accepting that we can stop carrying burdens of false beliefs in our thoughts and heart-center. Each step forward into the Light of Oneness helps us move forward into the truth of who we truly are … that of Unconditional Love and Light.

Hello and welcome Angel Meher. This topic of reconciliation and ultimate integration is fascinating and, I admit, a bit bewildering as to how to do this.

Angel Meher: it is indeed my pleasure to be addressing this topic as you say it, shedding much needed light and clarity for all.

Shall we begin then with a discourse on light and shadow?

Is there something more we should know and understand about light and shadow besides the light being about positive high-vibrations and shadow being more about negativity in any form?

Angel Meher: *Yes child there is much more to light and shadow. As with all things, there are degrees and layers, upon layers covering, weaving themselves into all facets of one's life.*

The brighter the light, the more difficult it can be to be seen by mere mortals who have not yet awakened. You have witnessed this phenomenon first-hand, have you not?

Yes, I have. When I was working a day-job as an Executive Administrative Assistant, there were some who never "saw" me even though I was right in front of them. It was as if they looked right past me.

The first several times this happened, I really thought people were being very rude. Now, of course, I realize it's all about the light and my inner-vibration.

Please explain more about integrating light and shadow.

Angel Meher: *Yes. This is a most critical and essential part of one's Earth Journey in physical form. Most are taught, as you were, that it is best to release, forget and walk away from that which is unpleasant or unwanted. Much like a memory that brings only a sense of renewed pain and sorrow, anger and frustration.*

Then when the unwanted, unpleasant memory re-surfaces, most feel they have failed in the healing and releasing only to re-live the memory as if is happening in the present moment.

The sole purpose of memories re-surfacing is to shed light from a different perspective. It is not always about the need to continue the healing process. There are of course those moments of memory re-surfacing that do require further healing energy.

When a memory re-surfaces "softly" as if "floating" up and out, nothing more is required than to acknowledge that memory as it continues its journey up and out from within one's inner-self.

Is this how we know we have begun the process of integrating those shadow parts of ourselves into the light and truth of who we truly are?

Angel Meher: *Yes. This is indeed a way, a small part of the overall integration process.*

Now I shall delve more deeply so that all may better understand the ways of transformation into Oneness.

There are many among you who seek only to distract and prevent as many as possible from entering and remaining in the light.

So many carry the burden of having failed at love, business or simply not being able to follow their purpose, that it quite literally prevents them from allowing that which is already theirs to manifest from Spirit into physical form.

Unless all who walk their path are truly ready to let go of that which is now behind them, both positive and negative, there is no true positive movement forward.

Yes, there are what can be named as positive forward movement, but it is often undone in the wake of dis-belief in one being worthy of receiving, maintaining, accumulating their heart wishes and desires.

That's very true. I've seen it in my life and in the lives of many of my clients until they are able to ascend to a higher-vibration energetically, changing at least one belief they held as truth.

Angel Meher: *This is the most common tripwire as the subconscious can only offer that which it has been given by the conscious mind time-and-time again.*

Many are so accustomed to remaining where they are told is their "place of being" there is little true effort to extricate themselves citing the difficulty of such a task when there are so many indications to the contrary which only continues the seemingly perpetual cycle of negative self-fulfilling prophecy.

That makes a lot of sense especially when something keeps happening and is seen as validation or confirmation that no matter what someone does to break a cycle of lack and limitation and the same struggles just keep showing-up.

Angel Meher: *It requires dedication in thought and deed to counter-act all previous thought and admonition from others. When one thought is repeated, it becomes a belief. A belief becomes a truth.*

A truth, even though that truth is an illusion, is difficult to root out at the core of one's inner-essence because it has been given the fertilizer of "proof" therefore a truth disguised as illusion, must be real.

With each realization of a truth which has been disguised and masquerading within illusion, is seen in the light of love and compassion and yes, forgiveness, then in that moment, the layers begin to peel away as they become transparent.

How does knowing this help us accept that light and shadow exist within us?

Angel Meher: *The knowing is the key to unlocking the mysterious ways of humanness you refer to as Ego. Dismantling illusion from truth allows one to set-down all that has been carried in their heart-center. All that does not serve serves only to cloud the true reality of Oneness.*

In truth, child, there is only light and love or fear and the shadows of darkness. In the shadows there is much fear disguised as anger, hurt, betrayal, forgiveness and deceit which surfaces as lack and limitation.

In the Light, even prior to full integration, there is cause for celebration. Celebrate those moments of non-resistance to that which continues to surface as reminders to let go.

Letting go does not, nor has it ever, signified a lack of control over one's self. It is quite the opposite. Letting go is the ceasing of being controlled by external events, experiences and those who would who see you staying small and insignificant in the shadows. Letting go is the ceasing of being controlled by internal negative thoughts and emotions.

In letting go, one ceases to carry burdens that were not theirs to carry, in letting go, true freedom surfaces to become a new belief in one's unlimited potential of Oneness.

What more need be said in the here and now? Integration is the true essence of healing in the Light of letting go all that no longer needs to be carried in thought or emotion.

If one's current reality is not to one's liking, there is but one recourse which is to change that which is carried in mind and heart and one's reality begins to change. This is true integration of light and shadow.

Wow. That is quite a lot to process. Is there anything more you wish us to know at this time Angel Meher?

Angel Meher: *We are complete. This discourse is now complete for these purposes.*

Thank you.

Angel Meher: *You are most welcome. I thank you for being such a willing vessel for these writings.*

Angel Gesele

Angel of Divine Life Purpose

One of the most difficult and challenging parts about being human --- in my humble opinion --- is figuring out what our Divine Life Purpose is. And then, once we know or think we know, how do we get to "that place" where we can actually start living and fulfilling our purpose AND trust prosperity and abundance are truly ours just by doing our part and following our inner-intuitive self and guidance from Angels?

This is what Angel Gesele is here to help us with. More specifically, this Angel helps us heal our transcendence from Spirit into physical form mentally, emotionally, energetically and Spiritually.

Angel Gesele will help you remember what was "forgotten" as we passed through the "Veil of Forgetfulness" and re-connect with our inner-intuitive Self.

Hello and welcome Angel Gesele. I feel so blessed to know what my Divine Life Purpose is and to be following my path to fulfilling that purpose. So many are not as fortunate ... how can we help thousands ... millions of people discover and then find the inner-courage and strength to follow their path with prosperity and abundance?

Angel Gesele: Hello and welcome child to the path you have chosen since the days of the beginning, long, long ago. You have come far along your path and are now reaching out to help others re-discover themselves in ways their Soul has yearned for as far as human memories allow the remembering.

What is the most common mis-understanding among the many?

The most common mis-conception is that many really feel and believe that if they knew why they were here, and then everything in their life would simply be resolved.

My sense of knowing is that we must first clear or at least begin to do the deep healing and forgiveness work around the false beliefs and illusions we've been taught to accept as truth of who we are and to live within the limited expectations of others opinions and judgements of what's truly possible for us to attain and achieve in this life-time.

Angel Gesele: This is indeed a very revealing concept about re-discovering one's Life Purpose while in human form. This is where we shall begin.

As you have said in your many teachings, one cannot expect to suddenly uncover their mystical purpose for being if they have not yet begun to decipher the many obstacles that begin with the transcendence from Spirit into their current physical form.

Allow me to explain further what is meant by transcendence from Spirit tonto physical form.

Yes, thank you. This will certainly help clear things up for many people.

Angel Gesele: Alright then, I shall begin thusly ... it is true all, each and every human has entered into a Soul Agreement of contract prior to the transformational process from Divinely Pure Soul Essence, into a "vessel" which is dark and crapped by *comparison. This "vessel" is the human body which is first housed within its Mother's womb for an extended period of time.*

At the moment of conception, the "vessel" is being prepared to receive the Soul. The Soul is also preparing to accept the initial limitation of what feels like confinement which is the total opposite of infinite and limitless expansion.

Infinite and limitless expansion is the true nature of every Soul whether housed in male or female "vessels."

Many Souls are simply unprepared for transcendence no matter if it is their first Earth Journey or it is their hundredth such journey. The "Veil of Forgetfulness" has a dual purpose of removing the trauma of transcendence once human life has ended and is once again returned Home.

There are of course those among you who's memories are intact which aide them in their current Earth Journey. Yet the "Veil of Forgetfulness" will not be denied its role in transcendence from Spirit into physical form for fear that more Souls wil choose not to incarnate for their agreed upon Earth Journeys.

How can we heal or begin to hear our transcendence?

Angel Gesele: *Ah, this is not so complicated a task as first imagined by the multitudes seeking the answers of their purpose, the true meaning of their existence in this place and time.*

Once the question arises from the depths of the inner-self, the way is being prepared for the honoring of the agreement to be of service in such a manner as to affect lasting change long after the Soul has returned back into Spirit from whence it came.

For many, the trauma of previous Earth Journeys is so great; they choose to remain unawakened because fear has erased the truth of light, unconditional love, and personal ascension while still remaining in their "Vessel."

Understanding need not be complete in this matter. What is requires is the willingness to accept transcendence as a truth. This in turn initiates healing on many levels, dissolving issues that have caused obstacles of connecting with the inner-intuitive Self for the remembering of one's Divine Life Purpose.

Let us be clear in these writings. One needs only begin the deep healing for the current human life, peeling back the first layers of "forgetfulness." It is then possible for the remembering to begin in earnest.

There appear to be multiple causes, yet there is only one root cause standing in the path of each Soul. You child have one such root cause.

I have known as far as I am able in this human life, that sense of being or having been abandoned, tainted everything. The healing has been much more difficult than I could possibly have imagined.

Angel Gesele: *Yet, you have managed to conquer this formerly crippling fear, have you not?*

Yes I have, for the most part. I say it that way because in those moments of extreme physical fatigue, my human-self or Ego-chitter chatter as I call it, can be triggered by a small incident, thought or emotion. In the past, I used to blame you ... all of you; my beloved Angels for not supporting me in ways I knew were possible.

There have been moments that being here was so overwhelming I yearned to go Home. In the summer of 2015, I made a decision to leave. I had been beaten down farther than I had ever experience. I no longer wanted to be here. I lay my head down and left my body. I was allowed to experience being Home for a few Earth day cycles then awoke once again to find myself back in this "vessel."

Major healing in the form of acceptance and complete and utter surrender is the way I was able to find, back to my true center. I am content to remain in physical form for as long as it is intended.

I am forever mindful of flowing with trust and faith and

learning more about the ways of being in human form, in service, assisting as many as possible, to discover their own innate uniqueness, walking their respective paths, connecting with Angels to live their purpose with prosperity and abundance.

Hopefully my Earth Journey helps others to find inner-courage and strength within themselves to live their purpose, following their path, no matter what circumstances they find themselves in at this very moment.

Angel Gesele: *This is indeed the way of things, child. You know this to be truth. Yet your humanness feels transparent in the sharing of all you have in these writings we create for all to further their determination of following their heart wishes, to living their Divine Life Purpose in its limitless fullness.*

The only limitation is that which is placed by one's conscious mind through fear and intimidation of failing. The possibility of failure prevents many from even beginning their inner-journey of healing enough to have a sense of energetic freedom to then delve into the remembering.

As the way is made clear through compassion for the inner and outer physical journey, one can them begin the process of receiving insights into who they are in this life and that which they have agreed upon to accomplish.

For many, this is a life-time of being of service. Being of service does not always mean becoming a healer through traditional or non-traditional avenues. One can be of service in a multitude of ways which serve in unique ways.

Some forms of service are tending the environment, protecting the many plants and animals on your world. Still others walk in silence, radiating light, love, compassion and humility.

You, child, are among the many who have chosen to allow your light to shine brightly as a wayshower no matter the seemingly surface based consequences. In truth, the one consequence is not following that which you know to be your truth, following guidance given to you by myself and my brethren.

For all, following the ways of human kind must be adhered to as wayshowers and of being in both realms simultaneously and remaining balanced, centered and grounded in the same moment.

It is not necessary to speak one's truth when one chooses to live from their truth. There are many who are affecting massive change in service to the multitudes who truly seek a better way.

There is little else for our purposes here. We have given much for those who choose to go within, re-connecting with their inner-intuitive Self to remember through healing their transcendence from Spirit into physical form, into their human "vessel."

With healing comes clarity, with clarity comes remembering. With remembering comes the fulfillment of one's Divine Life Purpose.

There remains nothing more at this time.

Thank you Angel Gesele, I feel my conscious mind reeling a bit with all you have shared with us.

Angel Gesele: *Yes this is indeed the reason we now stop this discourse. There is much given. The next awaits most patiently to be of service in this manner.*

Angel Domiel
Angel Prince of Majesty

Angel Domiel is an Angel who helps us face adversity with peace in our thoughts and love in our hearts. Even in the face of adversity, everything seemingly going "wrong" all at once, this kind, benevolent Angel asks us to open our eyes to the many blessings in our life.

As I was beginning to connect with Angel Domiel's energy, I 'wondered' softly to myself what "Majesty" symbolizes since Angels are love centered, not ego-driven. What I 'heard' as softly as I had 'wondered' is that Majesty means Grace Under Pressure. Speaking for me it's not always easy to do … come from love, peace, compassion and light.

Hello and welcome Angel Domiel. The Spiritual Path is not always an easy one, simple yes, easy, not so much.
Angel Domiel: This is the way of things child. You sense well, my eagerness to begin this most earnestly.
Yes. I do. How do you wish to proceed?
Angel Domiel: Ah, thank you for the opportunity to begin our discourse.

Your planet is riddled with subversion of the many truths of plenty for all. There are those among the many who contrive to control subjugation of their fellows by any means necessary. It is quite unfortunate to being in this negative manner and tone, yet it must first be addressed so we may begin the unraveling of the deep seated fears which tend to grip the hearts of humankind.

In this I must be crystal clear for there can be no confusion to the manner and tone which is to be taught here and now in this moment.

We often speak of forgiveness of the Self, forgiving of others and yet so many fight with themselves to hold onto their inner pain, feeling completely justified. What is not fully realized is the damage to one's Soul in the carrying of such deeply rooted anger.

This deep rooted anger attracts more of the same, for it cannot otherwise be. It is Law, pure and simple.

If I may interrupt for a moment?

Angel Domiel: *Yes, you may ask child.*

Thank you. How do we or can we break the cycle of negative attraction long enough to raise our inner-vibration and begin focusing our thoughts and emotions on peace and being in the Light?

Angel Domiel: *yes, I see now the dilemma. Allow me to explain further. Many times, the adversity at hand is the result of either past or current circumstances.*

The past has been in process to such a degree it has its own momentum and must be seen through to its natural conclusion. Meaning, once a tide of energy is in motion, unless and until there is a complete reversal with equal or greater positivity, there is what can be referred to as a lag time.

As a thought is focused upon, whether it is wanted or unwanted, energy is infused into that thoughts and its corresponding emotional energy stream.

Is this like trying to fix a leak, an energy leak before it gets out of control and becomes larger?

Angel Domiel: *Explain further please. I wish to be certain of my response to your query.*

Okay. When there is a small energy leak, it may go unnoticed because we are so busy with our lives and work. In the past I would ignore the subtle signs or nudges feeling so certain it was just my humans self causing resistance. At other times, I totally missed important guidance until it hit me smack upside the head and knocked me on my batukus.

By then it was almost always too late to stop the negative energy leak. All I could do was patch the breach as best I could and begin the healing process to prevent further damage. At others times, there was a slight delay in the backlash as the last of the negative issues surfaces to be dealt with.

Just the other day, an issue surfaced for me that was completely unexpected. It might seem minor to some reading these words, but, it was the final piece of an incident that had been resolved two weeks earlier. The internet connection had been terminated.

Thankfully, my 1st thoughts were how to work with this situation in case the connection wasn't fully restored for 24 hours. In the past, that would have triggered lots of fear, with me questioning everything. In a matter of minutes, the connection was fully restored.

Angel Domiel: *Yes, this speaks directly to our topic at hand. When one is consciously aware, connected to their truth, even in the face of adversity, there is peace.*

Let us move forward then to being or rising above, when all around you are fearful. You child, have witnessed many attempts to pull at you, in an effort to take for themselves or to hold you with them in the mire of negativity. This must be made very clear at this time. There is no judgement in our words, tone or manner.

This is unfortunately, a truth seen and experienced by many

Spiritual Leaders such as you. Walking in the Light has its gifts or advantages for ALL who choose to honor their path. The Light within acts as a deflector of negativity.

True, some negativity seeps through for there are those who are wholly committed to darkness and shadows, as those committed to the ways of Light.

How do we combat so much negativity without actually focusing on it and bringing it to us?

Angel Domiel: *When one focuses on the Light within, the space in between breaths, gives solace enough to break the cycle of negativity within thought and corresponding emotion. Meaning this child, no matter what faces you or appears on your path, taking the time to stop, breathe and retreat fully and completely into trust and faith that all is indeed well, regardless of surface appearances, this alone dissipates the potential magnitude of any situation. Does it not?*

Yes. The loss of connection could have thrown me off for an entire morning. Granted, it was not the way I had planned to spend my personal Spiritual studying. Sharing this with you now, I can see how it was an exercise in maintaining my sense of balance and inner-peacefulness about the situation.

Angel Domiel: *Was this not the way of forgiveness for those involved in creating the situation to begin with?*

Yes. When the situation first revealed itself, a few weeks ago, I did feel a sense of panic. I immediately reached out to my Spiritual family for help with prayer support knowing I needed help quickly or it could have spiraled out of control.

Angel Domiel: *Yes this is exactly the practice of Walking in the Light. You chose, consciously, to stay in a place of love, forgiveness and compassion and all was quickly resolved.*

Being in a State of Majesty when all around you are fearful of failure, letting go and of being fully seen is practiced. This is a life-long practice while being in human form as you well know beloved one.

Yes. When I get tired physically, mentally, emotionally and energetically, it takes focus to be mindful of my thoughts and emotions. It is not always easy to mindful in every moment.

Angel Domiel: *This is the way of the Light Path before ALL who choose to honor guidance received. There is magic, yet, there is shadow if one is not mindful of their steps upon the path. The way of the Spiritual Warrior is one of peace, love, harmony, conscious observance, and that of forgiveness. It is not the way of the Spiritual Warrior to be dis-honored or dis-regarded for all they have accomplished. The Humble of Spirit are those who see and choose to see past surface appearances.*

We are complete child.

Thank you Angel Domiel for all you have shared with us.

Angel Domiel: *It is I who is also grateful for this opportunity to be among those shedding Light for those on their Light Path to conscious mindfulness.*

Angel Uzzah
The Lord Is My Strength

There are many different kinds of strength, each with its own energetic vibration. Angel Uzzah is here to help us know when to speak our truth and when to remain silent.

Inner strength can often be seen by others to be weakness or not willing to stand your ground when it is quite the opposite. Compassion, kindness and humility can also be mistaken for allowing others to violate your boundaries.

Hello and welcome Angel Uzzah. This has been a difficult lesson for me to learn. Sometimes I still wonder if I have made the right decision, only to receive confirmation later that choosing to be silent was following guidance in that moment.

Will you help us understand this kind of inner-strength at deeper and higher levels of vibration?

Angel Uzzah: Yes, most assuredly. There is much to discuss for there are many who seek to hold Light Workers and Healers back from their destiny of fulfilling their purpose in freedom, without human imposed limitations.

How shall we first begin child? In which direction shall we proceed?

I would like to explore different kinds of inner-strength Light Workers and Healers face in those times of great awakening.

Angel Uzzah: *Which aspects in particular?*

Knowing when to speak and when to remain silent ... knowing when to stand our ground and when to step aside. I feel it is also very important to know how to protect ourselves when the Dark Side attempts to extinguish the flame within our heart-center.

Angel Uzzah: *Hmmm as you wish. Let us begin with those who use the darkness to gain trust. Do not underestimate those who hide among the shadows, they are as adept as many who walk on the Pathway of Light and Love.*

How can we protect ourselves without focusing on what we do not want to attract and manifest into our experience?

Admittedly, I have fallen victim to a few such individuals whose Soul Light was so dark; I could barely *see* the flame within their nearly coal-back heart-center.

I remember 'asking' for guidance only to have been led by those human individuals exactly where they intended. This really confused me because I kept getting reassurance from a trusted friend. Later, much later, after deep healing and forgiveness work on my part, did I realize the questions I asked were not specific enough.

There was a part of me that had a not-so-good feeling and yet I trusted the guidance. Not for one did I blame any of my beloved Angels; I only questioned how it happened ...

In a way, I felt like I had allowed myself to be scammed emotionally, mentally and even financially. The negative energy attachment from that person was incredibly powerful, if not for the protection of my beloved Angels, it could have been much worse.

How can we protect ourselves from this kind of deeply insidious darkness that weaves a type of mist, dulling our intuition and our connection to the Divine?

Angel Uzzah: We begin this by acknowledging there are limits to which the Veil of Darkness can be exposed as certain ones among you have practiced the Dark Magic many human life-times.

This is not cause for despair as it first appears there is no protection from those whose sole intention is to deceive. Quite the contrary, love is what saved you child from having been sucked into the depths of darkness, extinguishing the Light of Love within you.

You now see more clearly than any other comprehends. You, yourself have yet to fully comprehend the completeness within its totality of that which you truly possess. You see with such clarity, yet you still question the depth of your current levels of perception. At times, you feel these perceptions to be judgment, yet they are not.

You guard well against such judgments. The way in which you repeatedly receive the same impressions is the way you are reassured of all that is being given to you regarding others.

This, child, leads us directly into that State of Being or sense of knowing when to speak and when to remain silent.

Good. This isn't easy for some because they feel they must deliver messages they received regardless of circumstances or hurt that can be a result of certain messages having been given.

I do wonder why we are privy to very delicate information especially when it is not meant to be shared.

Angel Uzzah: First we shall discuss the knowing of silence and that which is to be spoken.

When one begins their inner-journey of Self-Reflection, there is much letting go, much healing and much inner-enlightenment. As one continues their inner-journey, more is revealed that may seem to appear as if by magical, mystical means.

All is a reflection of the inner-journey which then becomes reflected on the outside as physical manifestations both positive and negative.

You have sensed, quite early on, a knowing about potential events wished most deeply by some that would simply not occur. Have you not?

Yes, I have and still do. Why am I privy to these 'knowings' only to know I must remain silent in these matters?

Angel Uzzah: *The absence of malice in thought, emotion or action on the part of any who received these deeply-felt knowings is the very vibration in which these knowings are sensed and known to be truth. The purest of truths can, on the surface, appear to be human-based judgement.*

There are many more instances in which it is essential to deliver that which has been received. Still, there is a human-timing that is to be considered.

Please explain what you mean by human-timing?

Angel Uzzah: *Certainly. Yes, of course. Let us digress for a moment in an effort to become clear in this matter of considering human-based-timing.*

There are 3 Levels of Perception, 3 Levels of Knowing ...

* *that which is to be given immediately upon being received*
* *that which is to be held until directed to be given*
* *that which is to remain in the silence, unspoken*

All that we speak of here is these writings are part of the whole, that which is centered in strength.

The clearer one's channel to the Divine and that of my brethren and me, the easier it is for those among you who strive to create and maintain the clearest and purest of connections.

That which is given, yet to also know there is a slight delay before the giving of that which has been received, you child, have experienced many times over. You listen well knowing and trusting the moment to deliver these messages given to you for others.

Yes, this is true. Just recently, I started working very closely with like-minded Souls in other countries. There have been messages that have come to me and yet I just knew it wasn't yet time to give the message or offer prayers on their behalf.

Angel Uzzah: Many times, you and others perceive that which is to come. You no longer question this receiving on behalf of others. For yourself, you still discern these knowings not to be those fabricated by human consciousness.

Very true. Please help us ---and me --- understand why there are messages or knowings that are to remain in the silence, unspoken.

Angel Uzzah: Have we not already spoken of this?

Perhaps, but, if you would please address this a little bit more it would help. I don't feel this a burden, well, truth be told, sometimes it feels like I shouldn't know something like when it is so clear that someone is going down a wrong path that delays the manifesting of their dreams.

Angel Uzzah: Aright then let us delve more deeply so as to be clear.

As one, such as yourself, strives to be of service, uplifting as many as possible to realizing their purpose, it is inevitable in the energies surrounding those on their path, to receive the energy vibrations that one is bound and determined to follow simply because it was their right path to begin with.

What most fail to grasp, and this you have also experienced, is the pathway they are now following so earnestly, worked for them from a different point along their journey.

In this moment it is more of a compilation of the old and the new, rather than remaining where they were, vibrationally. Most, unfortunately, are not yet capable of seeing this truth. Therefore that which is perceived by you and others must remain in the silence, for if spoken aloud, though well intentioned, could cause more harm.

Should there come a time when such information is to be shared, there will be no doubt and it will be used in a most compassionate, loving manner as to support rather than destroy the recipient.

We have now addressed all that has been brought forth for clearer understanding on multiple levels of discernment of when to speak, when to remain silent and the standing of one's ground.

That which hides itself in the darkness, has also been discussed and revealed here.

Angel Uzzah, I have final question about protecting ourselves from those who live and thrive in the darkness.

Angel Uzzah: *Speak your question child, I shall answer this.*

How do we protect ourselves as much as possible from those who practice the Dark Arts?

Angel Uzzah: *Love. Coming from Love. Being Love. Radiating Love. Walking in Love. Speaking from Love. Love. It is not complicated. It is not that which comes easiest for it involves setting aside Human ego.*

Thank you Angel Uzzah for all you have shared with us.

Angel Uzzah: *You are most welcome for it needs to have been shared so all may know when to speak and when to honor that which is to remain in the silence.*

We are complete. Where there is love, there is no limitation only that which is limitless.

Angel Jehudiel
Divine Direction

Often we think we want to know everything about what is going to happen or could happen. The intention, or so we think, is to prepare ourselves for what is coming and what won't happen.

I used to think I could avoid certain relationships, skipping hurt and heartbreak and even disappointment. The truth, at least for me is, if I had truly known the many twists, turns, ups and downs my path would take me, I would have said "NO! NOT doing that!" then I would have slammed the door shut, boarded it and nailed it!

Imagine your life is like a tapestry with Divine Source and Angels guiding you each step of the way. So you look up at this tapestry called Life and all you see is a maze of colorful knots. There doesn't seem to be any rhyme or reason, to the pattern, just a massive maze that appears to be something less than beautiful or joyful.

Being willing to see beyond or through the seeming chaos of colored threads, is part of or Earth Journey.

Each day is a new beginning. As each day turns to dusk with the setting of the Sun, we can choose to release all cares and worries, or take them with us into our sleep.

It is important to remember where you have been, where you are and where you want to be. The tapestry, symbolizing your journey is a reflection of all that is now behind you. It's about being able to see the beauty through the maze of tangled, colored threads.

The Angel of Divine Direction, Jehudiel, has agreed to join us in conversation, to help us better understand our deep desire to know what's next in a world filled with uncertainty at nearly every turn.

Before we go any further, I feel the need to share with you that the Angels and I first started this channeling in January of 2016. It is now January of 2018. In the in-between-time, the Angels and I have published 4 books.

I share all this with you because you may notice a difference in the energy. I am not the same person I once was. My belief in myself, talents, skills and abilities have grown and expanded exponentially. My Inner-Light shines more brightly that even before. That alone has taken some getting used to.

Hello and welcome Angel Jehudiel.

Angel Jehudiel: *Hello child, I too have been waiting for this opportunity to speak with you in delivering this most important messaging about one's Divine Direction.*

Know it could not have been completed any sooner as what is now being asked of you is greater than ever before. There is a deep-seated need for the many to have a deeper, wider understanding about the tapestry of their Life Path as they walk their journey in physical form regardless of gender or culture.

Thank you for your patience and understanding.

Angel Jehudiel: *It is we who are beholding to you for having agreed to speak with us in this manner. It is no small feat that is asked of you.*

Thank you for your reassurance.

Angel Jehudiel: Let us begin. There is much to discuss. What is it you would ask of me beloved one.

Please explain what Divine Direction is.

Angel Jehudiel: Ah yes. There is much confusion about one's Divine Direction in this life.

In essence, there are one-in-the-same, yet they are not.

I am confused, they are the same, but they are different?

Angel Jehudiel: Yes.

May we please discuss each individually and then explore the similarities?

Angel Jehudiel: Yes. So be it. Divine Direction is that which is manifested through countless choices, decision and actions both taken and those not taken.

There are many thoughts behind each action taken. Just as there are many thoughts behind each action not taken. Each thought, each action is manifested through steps both taken and those not taken. A direction is the sum total of decisions, actions and thoughts.

Opportunities to choose differently or to continue on as before are presented consciously. Some opportunities are offered as validation of decisions made. Others are offered to serve as reminders if that which is no longer desired.

In many instances, one chooses to remain in a well-worn direction because it is known, not necessarily wanted. Direction can be changed and modified at any time and as often as is required to be fully aligned with one's Life Purpose.

Divine Direction is a course or pattern that is laid out before you. There is always choice in how one's Life Purpose is fulfilled.

I am beginning to understand how Divine direction and Life Purpose are similar and yet different.

Angel Jehudiel: Good. How else shall I serve thee here?

Well. I am curious about our need to KNOW what's ahead of us. For example, earlier today, during a reading I was giving a new client, she wanted to know exactly what was going to happen in two years.

I explained that the energy was going to be very different and that I was only able to share guidance with the energy as it is in this moment. What she really wanted was a guarantee of what would happen and when.

Angel Jehudiel: *This, as you know beloved one, is not possible as the variables are far too many to consider in this instance and in those of countless others.*

Yes. I do understand. Still, it is frustrating and sometimes very irritating to be given guidance when I journal and it doesn't come to pass. Sometimes the manifested reality falls incredibly short of what was promised. This makes it difficult to continue having faith and trust in that which is given, please help me understand this.

Angel Jehudiel: *Yes. It often happens; guidance and manifested reality are mis-aligned. This is a way of things. Not always mind you, still it does persist in its outcome.*

Why?

Angel Jehudiel: *It is simple child. The conscious mind has a very different agenda. It insists on having that which is most important to you weave itself through the many knots and backtracking of events long since forgotten and buried in the Psyche.*

Memories are much like land-mines wanting to be exposed and diffused through love and forgiveness. Most often, through no fault of yours, these memories tend to leak energy in the form of negative messages of self-worth, ability and degree of worthiness upon your part. Once identified, these memories are instantaneously diffused.

There are memories that require more than acknowledgement. I teach my clients to write letters about their experiences and then burn them. I use this same technique myself to help with forgiveness, healing and releasing the energy.

Angel Jehudiel: *This is most efficient.*

Is there anything else we can do to help us release memories that have caused so much hurt or anger? I know it's not healthy on any level for us to keep unwanted energy of any kind within or heart and mind.

Angel Jehudiel: *This is indeed a most important topic. Without continuous clearing, healing and releasing, you cannot completely follow the Divine Direction. Being blocked causes great delay in the fulfilling of your purpose.*

Unfulfillment leads to disappointment and frustration which often results in despair. You, child, have faced this feeling of great despair many times, have you not?

Yes. Many times I just quit. Even so, there was always a part of me that knew I would continue once the 'storm' had passed. Each time y'all waited patiently till I was once again open enough to accept healing, support and encouragement from you.

Angel Jehudiel: *Yes. Those passing moments are most difficult for us, my brethren and me, to witness. There is little else that can be done in times of great trials.*

Are those kinds of dark moments, which sometimes stretch into hours, days or even weeks, really a necessary part of Spiritual Expansion?

Angel Jehudiel: *Think of it in these terms of needing to clear out very deep levels of mind, heart and Soul. It is a battle between the truth of who you are and that of the conscious mind, for control and that freedom to flow along your path with grace and ease.*

The conscious mind fears its own death unless it has full and complete control over your every waking moment. This depth of control stifles your Inner-Spirit to the point of extinction. Hence the lack of Light that seen in the eyes of many who have chosen the path of conformity. Conformity is not the enemy, necessarily. Conformity is a path choice. It is the opposite of Divine Direction.

There is much to be discovered as you continue the work given to you. There is always choice in the completion and choices made along the way.

There is no right path. Each must choose for themselves, how they will fulfill their Life Purpose. In this, they find the true compass for their Divine Direction.

If there are no other questions, we are now complete.

No, there are no other questions. Thank you for such an enlightening conversation about Divine Direction and our Life Path.

Angel Jehudiel: *You are most welcome beloved one. I shall leave you now. There are others of my kind awaiting the sharing of messages and guidance.*

Angel Omniel
Oneness of Spirit

Oneness is an elusive, vague concept of being in a State of Grace. It is like experiencing a dimension filled only with peace and contentment, while you are fully aware of your surroundings. We are a part of something so much larger that the conscious mind allows us to accept and believe.

Angel Omniel is amazingly powerful. This Angel is also incredibly soft and unassuming, almost as if there is no intensity that is definable. His insights are going to help us have a better, clearer understanding about Oneness of Spirit and how to experience it more often.

Hello and welcome Angel Omniel. It is indeed an honor and a pleasure to be connecting with you here in this moment. What is Oneness of Spirit, how do we experience this seemingly elusive State of Being?

Angel Omniel: *It is with great anticipation to cones with you as well Child of Light. We shall begin by answering the question of what it means t be in such a State of Being that all things feel as if there is no division between time and space.*

It is more a sense of nothingness as well as fully comprehending all things in the same moment. You have experiences many such moments more often these past days and weeks. Is this not truth?

Yes, I have, just this morning. It is such a delish feeling to be completely at peace. It is almost as if time stands still and everything has more dimension to it.

Angel Omniel: *Explain further. You clarify well your experiences for others.*

Thank you, the dimension, it's like there are layers of energy that stretch without distortion. It usually happens while I'm journaling in my beautiful garden. The edges of plants and objects are sharper and clearer. The whole space is just so serene. It's not easy putting into words because it almost defies description.

Angel Omniel: *This is accurate. A State of Being in its purest essence defies words. This is the beauty and difficulty of Oneness of Spirit. There are many facets and there is only one. What else puzzles?*

How can we attain or experience Oneness of Spirit? Isn't in this space of nothingness and everything that Miraculous Manifestation occurs?

Angel Omniel: *Yes indeed this is so. Yet, be forewarned, once the outcome is sought as the sole purpose of attaining Oneness of Spirit, that which is sought shall remain forever elusive.*

In the wanting, there is need. In the need there is lack. In the absence of lack is ALL in its purest form of purest physical manifestation. It matters not what has been asked. In the asking, all is given, every time without fail. There are no exceptions. Ask and you shall receive. Seek and you shall find. Knock and the door shall be opened to you.

Each has infinite choice to accept or deny that which has been asked.

I believe this Universal Truth. With every fiber of my being and yet I have experienced countless disappointments.

Angel Omniel: Yes, this is a truth. There is no denying there are many, perhaps countless instances upon which can be counted in the non-manifestation that which is deeply desired.

Where there is one involved, the way is made easier. When there is another involved, other than that of one's self involved, there is a dance of energies, and that of circumstances which color, speed and thus impede the delivery from pure energy into physical form.

Is this now understood more clearly?

Yes, thank you. How does being in a State of Oneness help us allow everything that is already in our Spiritual Escrow account show up for us?

Angel Omniel: It is a form of alignment. One often hears statements of Divine Order, when the time is right and even when the Stars in the Heavens are aligned, this is when all manifests. All things, both great and small, come to pass when there is no resistance to what is desired.

There is no desire to great or too small to be worthy of taking physical form exactly as it is requested or better. All that is requested of those doing the requesting, is a clear, steady, unwavering vision and belief it has already come to pass.

So alignment, meaning our energy, thoughts and emotions, are what determine the when of what we desire to fully manifest for us?

Angel Omniel: Yes, this is so.

All we really need to do is stay out of our way mentally, emotionally and energetically?

Angel Omniel: Yes, this is so. It is also quite necessary for one to have a sense of irrefutable knowing, regardless of outward appearances. Outward appearances are to some, the one true reality. In so believing this to be their truth, the reality must indeed remain the same for it is what is fed in both mind, thought, and deep within the heart space.

It requires concerted effort to side-step that which has been deeply ingrained from birth through oral history and actions witnessed.

One can indeed overcome any and all obstacles set before them. This requires more than decision. This also requires seeing, feeling, acting, speaking and believing differently to such depths that all prior beliefs are obliterated. Once an illusion has been obliterated, the vision of what is desired can take root, grow, loom and then flourish; bearing all that has been and is promised through vision, guidance messages received.

As each illusion of lack, no matter the manner in which it has shown itself, has been revealed and subsequently demolished, more Light, more alignment is experienced.

In alignment all things are possible for there is no resistance. Without resistance, all happens in the blink of an eye. The unexpected happens as if by magic. The magic is in the Oneness of Spirit.

It is simply recognized, first, that which is truly Divine within and also that which if Divine within others. This is the way of attaining Oneness of Spirit.

Is there more that is needed upon this most timely subject matter?

No. There are no other questions thank you very much for all you have shared with us.

Angel Omniel: *You make this possible child. Through you we have a voice as bright as light.*

Thank you, Angel Omniel. Your words humble me.

Angel Omniel: *There is true Light, Passion and Love within you for our combined works on these matters bringing insights where they are much needed.*

We are complete the next awaits.

Gauri'el Ishlila
Angel Prince of the East

There are countless opportunities to choose differently, to truly step into, claim and own our unique brilliance. We talk about new beginnings by letting go of the old ways of thinking feeling and being. Yet, how many of us truly allow ourselves to completely take that next step off the edge of everything we have ever known, into the seeming nothingness of trust and faith? This is something I am consciously working with every single day.

This amazing Angel, Gauri'el Ishlila, is going to help us do more of what we came here to do by giving us insight into how to bridge Heaven and Earth within our very Soul.

Hello and welcome Angel Guari'el Ishlila. It is a pleasure to be connecting with you here and now in this moment.

Angel Guari'el Ishlila: *It is I child who is most welcoming this time of sharing the deeper understandings of facing the Self in all its aspects whether they be positive or negative as judge by the conscious collective.*

What do you mean the conscious collective?

Angel Guari'el Ishlila: *The conscious collective is a mass* *gathering of energies that now has its own magnetic attraction regardless of the overall vibrational frequency.*

Can you give us an example?

Angel Guari'el Ishlila: *Yes, most certainly this I shall do now. It is a most important aspect of understanding from whence certain patterns of thoughts and accompanying emotions originate.*

Long ago, and as each new generation comes into being, there are specific patterns of thought that have become beliefs which have ultimately transformed into truths. Not all truths are Universal Truths. There are merely those thoughts and beliefs which have been practiced and are now believed to be truths simply because of their mere existence through the Ages of Time.

Like the belief that to be Spiritual, truly Spiritual, one must be willing to do without or give to others without regard to their own welfare?

Angel Guari'el Ishlila: *Yes, this is very much so. These current times are unlike any other in the history of the Ages, and yet, there are many similarities among the Spiritual Advancement of Humankind.*

I often help my clients understand this concept of being self-focused by taking care of themselves first. It is about making themselves a priority so they do not get so energetically overwhelmed, they give up or burn out and quit.

Angel Guari'el Ishlila: *Yes, this is most distressing to all concerned. Each time a Light stops shinning, the collective diminishes. The converse is also true, as another steps out of the shadows of denying who they are, the collective becomes brighter.*

Being in the Light is about so much more than opening one's mind and heart to the truth of their ultimate reason for being in physical form. Yes, it is about the Human expectation and yet it is not at all as that is finite experience in and of itself.

It is about connecting with the Ancient Texts, renewing one's Spirit amid the seeming chaos that is spewed out to the masses in every moment of every day. To be able to rise above the conscious collective is not to deny there is mass assumption and judgement. You often speak of acknowledging that which you observe and moving your perceptions beyond the surface appearances.

Yes, I do teach this awareness. It is something I practice. Sometimes I catch myself judging appearance maybe it is because there is soooo much 'judgement energy' surrounding a person or situation.

Angel Guari'el Ishlila: *Yes this is indeed a truth. Energy has its own magnetic field. Do you not at times catch yourself responding in ways that are not of your Soul vibration?*

Yes. I do wonder at times where 'that' came from. I do my best to let go and be more aware of judgment before it fully forms in thought, energy or emotion.

Angel Guari'el Ishlila: *Yes, this is the way of things. One way to dissolve a seeming obstacle such as judgement is to recognize it, releasing it immediately and sending love from the heart. This is not to say denial of one's reality is the answer. Reality is created moment by moment for some. For others, they are to simply follow a path, a pre-determined path regardless of their own desires for a complete dissolution of the current reality to create that which burns deep within their Soul.*

This subject of the conscious collective is now complete. What else shall we discuss?

Well, one of the affirmations I work with every day is "I walk boldly up to the Lion on my pathway and find Angels clearing the way." It is one I learned from Florence Scovel Shinn, a truly remarkable Light.

Angel Guari'el Ishlila: *That she was as she was Divinely Guided among the adversity of her times and that which was socially accepted. The path of the Enlightened is not always paved with gemstones. There are obstacles of every imaginable sort. That is our purpose, the sorting and clearing of obstacles on* your behalf. True, this may at times seem as though, we, my brethren and I, are unseeing, unhearing, unknowing and simply absent. This is far from the truth and yet many suffer. But I digress child. What is your inquiry on this subject of facing the Self?

What you just shared with us, needed to be said. I have felt many times that I was completely on my own trying to figure things out, like my connection wasn't god enough or clear enough. I do know this is an illusion.

My question about facing ourselves is how do we face a fear so BIG without it consuming us on every level possible?

Angel Guari'el Ishlila: *Ah yes this is indeed worthy of great discussion here.*

Facing the Self is the way of dissolving that which carries within it great power over truth. In truth, there is only that which is Love and Light. There is nothing to fear except that which is feared. Allow me a moment to explain further.

Yes, please. I have an understanding of this concept. I would really like to understand this more.

Angel Guari'el Ishlila: *Ah yes, then we shall continue. Imagine, if you will, being at the shore's edge of a great lake. Now then, take a step forward. The water is icy cold. So the foot is then drawn back. Once again, the foot is extended in to the icy water. It is now known so the initial shock is less than a moment ago, is it not?*

Yes.

Angel Guari'el Ishlila: *It is the same facing one's fear, no matter how great or small. It said, light from a single candle illuminates an entire room. No shadow remains. By acknowledging a fear, its power is greatly lessened; fully opening the mind to all possibilities both positive and negative, dissolving immediately, the power of fear. Embracing fear with an open mind and heart filled with love, regardless of any seeming obstacles, raises the Spirit within beyond the level of fear, thus erasing doubt.*

As fear is dissolved through Light and Love, a way is revealed and the solution becomes known. Action is then required on the part of the Self whether it be through some physical action or through forgiveness.

The acceptance of that which faces the Self is the way through that stich is in front and center on one's path. Clearing of obstacles is through Light, acceptance and love. Only through Love, are all things possible.

I find that writing out what I am feeling really helps me release fear energy the quickest. After I finish writing, I burn it, watching the flames turn paper into smoke and dissolving into thin air, releasing energy into the Universe for healing and transmutation.

Angel Guari'el Ishlila: *This is a most efficient use of all energies on all levels as this is a most loving way to stand, facing fear.*

If there is nothing more or me, we are concluded on this matter.

Just one more question please.

Angel Guari'el Ishlila: *Yes child, speak now your request.*

Thank you. How then, does facing fear help us bridge Heaven and Earth within our Soul?

Angel Guari'el Ishlila: *Very good. Yes, this is so on every level of understanding.*

As the Self is faced, fear is dissipated, vibration from the very depth of heart and Soul are then raised, bridging the gap of gear and love itself. Where Love is, there is no fear. Where fear is absent, Love reigns supreme in all its glorious radiance. Love is the bridge bringing Heaven and Earth together as one within the very Soul of the Self.

This is now understood?

Yes. Thank you.

Angel Guari'el Ishlila: We are now complete.

This completes the first of five volumes for *Conversations with Angels*. Our next channelings are focused on Prosperity and Abundance.

Much Love, Light, Peace and Purpose,

the Angel Lady Terrie Marie, D.Ms.

Ready to Become a Mover and Shaker of Your Reality?

Get Your Free Easy to Follow Guide
Angels Success and Prosperity:

Become a Mover and Shaker of Your Reality

* 3 Reasons WHY People Fear Success and Spirituality Keeping Them Out of Alignment with Their Dreams, Goals and Deepest Desires

* 3 Inner-Game 'Tells' That Keep You From Breaking through to Success and Prosperity

* Prosperity and Success Angels You Can Connect with Today to Help You Get to that Next Level and Stay There!

http://angeldreamteam.com

About the Angel Lady Terrie Marie, D.Ms.

The Angel Lady Terrie Marie, D.Ms., is a highly sensitive Angel Intuitive Specialist helping Empaths Worldwide tap into their **Divine Birthright of having it ALL,** easily accessing their Intuitive Empathic Skills, Angels and Spirit.

Blasting through sub-conscious patterns of resistance and **dissolving negative self-talk are KEY steps** in clearing your path to being seen and magnetic. Following their Inner GPS, her clients get clarity they need to live their dreams doing what they love most.

As a Best-Selling Author and Intuitive Empath Coach, she radiates Spiritual Presence, Unconditional Love and compassion, as **she teaches life-transforming skills,** easy-to-use techniques, in practical ways that work quickly and easily.

Terrie Marie **helps her clients transform their lives** and their Spiritual Businesses from the inside out **in miraculous ways.**

www.ingramcontent.com/pod-product-compliance
Lightning Source LLC
LaVergne TN
LVHW051848080426
835512LV00018B/3139